Eco-Freud

ALSO AVAILABLE FROM BLOOMSBURY

Dump Philosophy, Michael Marder
Dust, Michael Marder
Groundless Existence, Michael Marder

Eco-Freud
From A to Z

Michael Marder

BLOOMSBURY ACADEMIC
LONDON • NEW YORK • OXFORD • NEW DELHI • SYDNEY

BLOOMSBURY ACADEMIC

Bloomsbury Publishing Plc, 50 Bedford Square, London, WC1B 3DP, UK
Bloomsbury Publishing Inc, 1385 Broadway, New York, NY 10018, USA
Bloomsbury Publishing Ireland, 29 Earlsfort Terrace, Dublin 2, D02 AY28, Ireland

BLOOMSBURY, BLOOMSBURY ACADEMIC and the Diana logo are trademarks of
Bloomsbury Publishing Plc

First published in Great Britain 2025

Copyright © Michael Marder, 2025

Michael Marder has asserted his right under the Copyright, Designs and Patents Act, 1988,
to be identified as Author of this work.

Cover design: Ben Anslow
Cover images © AdobeStock / Getty Images

All rights reserved. No part of this publication may be: i) reproduced or transmitted in any form, electronic or mechanical, including photocopying, recording or by means of any information storage or retrieval system without prior permission in writing from the publishers; or ii) used or reproduced in any way for the training, development or operation of artificial intelligence (AI) technologies, including generative AI technologies. The rights holders expressly reserve this publication from the text and data mining exception as per Article 4(3) of the Digital Single Market Directive (EU) 2019/790.

Bloomsbury Publishing Plc does not have any control over, or responsibility for, any third-party websites referred to or in this book. All internet addresses given in this book were correct at the time of going to press. The author and publisher regret any inconvenience caused if addresses have changed or sites have ceased to exist, but can accept no responsibility for any such changes.

A catalogue record for this book is available from the British Library.

A catalog record for this book is available from the Library of Congress.

ISBN: HB: 978-1-3505-3842-9
PB: 978-1-3505-3843-6
ePDF: 978-1-3505-3844-3
eBook: 978-1-3505-3845-0

Typeset by RefineCatch Limited, Bungay, Suffolk
Printed and bound in Great Britain

To find out more about our authors and books visit www.bloomsbury.com
and sign up for our newsletters.

Contents

Preface vii

A Anxious states 1

B Biodiversity conundrums (with an eye to the death drive) 9

C Civilization and its (presumed) anti-ecologism 17

D Dump, Defecation 25

E Environment, "external world," eco-psycho-analysis 31

F Fetishism and the climate 39

G Geo-psycho-analysis 45

H Hysteric conversions between organismic and ecological bodies 53

I Inhibitions: of ecological thinking and/in action 61

J Jokes and their relation to the eco-crisis 69

K Kissing and knowing 75

L Libidinal ecologies 81

M Melancholy variations 87

N Negative ecology 95

O Obsessive self-blame 103

P Plants and psychoanalysis 109

- **Q** Queer ecology, Freud-style 119
- **R** Rats, horses, wolves, and other animals 127
- **S** Sadism and the sentience of other-than-human beings 135
- **T** Trauma extensions 143
- **U** Uncanniness: leaving, coming back home, and leaving again with ecology 151
- **V** Vultures, kites, and other ani-things 159
- **W** Wish fulfillment and green dreams 165
- **X** Xylophone magic: echoes and eco's 171
- **Y** Yes-saying: affirmations and the limits of analysis 177
- **Z** Zoophilia vs. zoephilia 183

Notes 189

Preface

This is Freud's time: just when "the father of psychoanalysis" has been all but written off, his agile, living thinking and method become more important than ever. To be more precise, this is the time of the weird (perhaps, the weirdest) Freud who finds the anachronistic structures of past ages preserved in our psyches as though nothing had changed; who, still further afield, locates the entire development of humankind, the history of life on earth, and a succession of geological epochs in a miniaturized and sped-up fashion within the story of a single human being; who, beyond the pleasure principle, discovers the death drive in the temptation of absolute regression to a state devoid of all tension in the inorganic prelude of organic existence; who revives the ancient thinking of *eros*, translated into a drive toward the aggregation of multiplicities, whether human or not; who locates the origins of time-perception in the rhythmic acts of reality testing by the antennae-like apparatus of consciousness, which is but a small retractable part of the unconscious . . .

I could continue the list almost indefinitely. But my point is that the bio-physio-psycho-logical, ecological, geological, and planetary aspects of Freud's works, long overlooked or dismissed as sheer eccentricities, are finally coming to the fore as the astute features of psychoanalysis uniquely befitting current vectors of thought. As I strive to demonstrate in what follows, in addition to the invaluable contributions "eco-Freud" makes to the ecological broadening and deepening of the psyche, this conceptual figure—this up until now hardly recognized persona of psychoanalysis—holds essential insights on how to relate to, deal with, counteract, and transform the ever-worsening situation of planetary devastation. The two aspects of "eco-Freud" are effectively inseparable from one another and from the continuing relevance of psychoanalysis in the contemporary agonized and antagonized world ablaze and in ruins.

To be sure, the psychoanalytic reckoning with planetary devastation is barely beginning. Strictly economic explanations for suicidal unwillingness to reduce CO2 emissions, to discontinue the massive and still growing global generation of plastics and their derivatives, to transition to alternative sources and meanings of energy, or to implement a less environmentally harmful mode of production and consumption are sorely insufficient.[1] (Similarly insufficient are the financial, compensatory solutions to the climate crisis, framed in terms of debt.) Wars raging over land and sea, home to limited and dwindling resources, combine genocide with ecocide, much more damaging than the scorched earth strategy of old. Battles to control heavily mined, flooded, toxicity-laced, permanently hostile terrains, waterways, shifting coastal areas, and the seabed undermine the very rational calculative logic, which could account for such bloody conflicts. The pursuit of a "green economy" and "green energy" prompts governments to chop down hundreds of thousands of mature trees in order to install solar power farms. The madness driving these events and processes is glaring.

Despite a rapid amassing of discourses around energy, for instance, and despite the emergence of new academic fields, such as "energy humanities," there is no interrogation of the *senses* of energy and consequently of its scope beyond powering our appliances and gadgets, means of transport, factories, and online activities. Wherever one looks, the desirability and undesirability of its different sources are in the spotlight, rather than the extension of the extractive-destructive practices to knowledge production, to the economies of abstract value (i.e., capital), to systems of valuation in general, to bodies, minds, and worlds.[2] From energy policy planning to activist organizing, the feeling of urgency, of running out of time to save a livable world, is the usual explanation for the short shrift the question of energy receives. Such an explanation is not to be taken at face value, even by those who sincerely cling to it. Like all rationalizations, it is symptomatic of repression, the substitution of a repressed idea by another, more acceptable one (SE 14: 182).[3]

The key word here is *symptomatic*. If the question of energy fails to reach deep enough to indicate that nuclear fission and the utilization of fossil fuels belong to the same energy paradigm with the desire to extract surplus value from labor or to burn as many calories as possible in a workout, it is not due to intellectual incapacity. Lacunae in research and inquiry, theory and practice, critical analysis and synthetic vision are symptoms of resistances, the dams erected by psychological repression, which lets all these endeavors go this far and no further. They block the questioning impulse. That is why—to return to our example—the revaluation of energy sources proceeds largely by (unfree) association: fossil fuels are affectively charged as "bad" and renewables are perceived as "good," even though some of the latter, such as bio-ethanol, are more environmentally destructive overall than the former.

Like any symptomatology, that of the climate crisis presents symptoms in a twisted, distorted form with respect to what they are symptomatic of, what they are unable to express less obliquely due to the power of repression. Further, the symptomatology is quite stable on both sides of the barricades, among climate skeptics and climate activists alike. Although the values "good" and "bad," which members of each group attribute to fossil fuels, are diametrically opposed, they do not budge from the predesignated field, in which this or that energy source will be adopted or spurned. Without contemplating the dangers of nuclear energy, the unresolved storage problems of spent nuclear rods, and, above all, the co-belonging of nuclear and fossil fuels in an overarching extractive-destructive energy paradigm, intergovernmental bodies, governments, and activists throw their support behind—and fall into the trap of—a particular source of energy. Again, the success of the nuclear lobby with political decision-makers and passionate anti-fossils climate activists is a sign not only of their superb marketing and rhetorical skills, but also of the stable symptomatology, which we have just started to address.

Is it sufficient for experts and visionaries to issue warnings about the disastrous course on which we are at the moment? A philosophy of warnings, currently being elaborated by Santiago Zabala, seems more necessary than ever.[4] It is replete with hermeneutical suggestions on how to interpret the alarm signals emitted by a welter of crises humanity and the planet are embroiled in. What is missing from the otherwise timely philosophy of warnings is a more precise figure of their addressee. Who is being warned? To whom are the many mutually reinforcing warnings addressed? Evidently, the addressee is the conscious subject, capable of assessing risks and mitigating them with recourse to rational decision-making, comparisons of the present with a plausible future, and so on. Nonetheless, warnings often fall on deaf ears of the unconscious, which may, in fact, subvert a rational course of action and endanger survival.[5] A more precise question, then, is: How to speak to the unconscious? In what language and with which images? Is it possible to warn the unconscious (which, as Freud has it, is unaware of the passage of time) about an *impending* disaster, about a future that is different from the past and the present, and that sends its desperate signs to this very present?

Cosimo Schinaia's recent *Psychoanalysis and Ecology: The Unconscious and the Environment*[6] is a welcome step toward tackling the psychological issues embedded in some of the prevalent responses to the environmental crisis. But, as is to be expected of a practicing analyst—and Schinaia is one—many of the astute observations in the book have to do with individual reactions, including clinical cases, while few touch upon the underlying unconscious complexes that are quasi-universal. In my *The Phoenix Complex: A Philosophy of Nature*,[7] I have sketched out the outlines of one such complex, in my opinion more widespread and older than the Oedipus complex, or indeed any other identified by Freud and subsequent psychoanalysts. The crux of the Phoenix complex is that, at least since the Neolithic period, human beings around the world have related to their own bodies, societies, ideas, and other-than-human nature as though they were the miraculous creatures of the ancient myth of the Phoenix: mortal, yet also immortal; prone to be reborn from the ashes of their own destruction. The unconscious framing of finite being as a source of potentially infinite being, projected into the future, prevents the Phoenix subjects from coming to terms with absolute finitude (or "finite finitude"), irrecoverable in any subsequent iteration of existence. An obvious conclusion is that until we untangle the Phoenix complex—a process that will, of necessity, be long and uneven, given the entrenchment of this complex in the structures of the unconscious—meaningful change is not likely to happen.

Pivotal as the Phoenix complex is, it does not stand alone as a barrier, preventing changes of attitudes and behaviors toward life and the living, toward the exhaustion of species and ecosystems, toward energy production and consumption, among other facets of the environmental crisis. A fresh look, at once panoramic and very close, at the symptoms and the multiple unconscious causes of the current predicament is in order. To this end, psychoanalytic theories may be collected in a diagnostic toolkit of cultural tendencies and of political, institutional, economic, and individual responses to the disastrous state of environmental affairs. More importantly, psychoanalysis may point the way to a meta-philosophical examination of the ideational background, context, and implications of ecological devastation as themselves symptomatic of something else, something yet to be identified, indexed, and dealt with.

The examination I call for as part of the psychoanalytic reckoning with ecological devastation is irreducible to a purely academic exercise. It implies lifting psychological resistances that render certain options, assemblages, images, and logics unthinkable and unimaginable, while others appear so obvious as to be immune to questioning and criticism. It also urges eco-activists, who sharply feel the environmental crisis, grieve the loss of biodiversity, and decide to do something about it, to combine their actions with *persistent self-analysis*, to tackle the other—including the despised, rejected, or repressed other—in themselves. The arduous and essentially incomplete (hence, requiring patient recommencement) endeavor of lifting resistances generates a powerful resistance of its own, prompting the rejection of, and negative transference toward, the person or triggering event responsible for this endeavor. I fully expect that some of this negativity will ricochet toward me, but I still consider the effort worthwhile. This late in the game, the stakes are too high to try and dodge the difficulties inherent in promoting *self*-understanding, without which climate activism loses much of its edge.

When eco-anxiety and depression become prevalent among children, adolescents, and young adults; when, at peak cynicism, oil-producing countries and CEOs host global climate summits; when deforestation and desertification, accompanied by the loss of plant and animal species, accelerate at an unprecedented rate; when environmental trauma, understood as an external event having a lasting psychological or physical impact on an individual, gives way to environment *as* trauma—then it is important to take a hard look at the outside world as well as inside the psychic realm. Whether brushing it off as a waste of time synonymous with *in*action or secretly concerned that it would pose a threat to their otherwise unshakable convictions, activists as a rule avoid introspection. A friendly reminder I want to issue is that, far from narcissistic navel-gazing, the introspective stance is indispensable to a sound activist practice and to its goal of salvaging livable environments for human and other-than-human beings. To paraphrase Marx's eleventh thesis on Feuerbach, the point is to change the world by psychoanalytically reinterpreting both the world and ourselves.

A

Anxious states

Eco-anxiety and eco-depression are some of the most prevalent attitudes toward the environmental crisis, particularly as experienced by the younger generations around the world.[1] How is it possible not to be anxious in the face of catastrophic climate change and the already happening as well as impending collapse of ecosystems around the world? But it is because eco-anxiety is such a widespread affect and because of what it holds in store for the possibility of action that we need to examine it under a psychoanalytic microscope.

Between the final years of the nineteenth century and the *New Introductory Lectures on Psychoanalysis* of the 1930s, Freud dedicated a great deal of his writings to the problem of anxiety. With time, his views on the subject changed, sometimes quite drastically, even if a few basic insights persisted. One of these is the idea that the object of anxiety is vague and indefinite, in contrast to that which is feared. Neurotic symptoms are formed, Freud claims in the 1926 study "Inhibitions, Symptoms, and Anxiety," in order to avoid anxiety—"they bind the psychical energy which would otherwise be discharged in anxiety" (SE 20: 144).[2] Phobias have the same function as neurotic symptoms, in that they substitute for the indefinite (and, as a result, unmanageable) wave of anxiety a circumscribed object to be afraid of: "A phobia generally sets in after a first anxiety attack has been experienced in specific circumstances, such as in the street or in a train or in solitude. Thereafter the anxiety is held in ban by a phobia, but it re-emerges whenever the protective condition cannot be fulfilled" (SE 20: 128).

The logic of substituting the indefinite with the definite trigger of negative affect is rather expensive, requiring a constant investment of energy into the supplanting of anxiety with phobias and the maintenance of "the protective condition," which ends up impeding one's everyday life. In its pure indefinite state, eco-anxiety corresponds to the vague and all-embracing object it is anxious about, namely the loss of a livable environment or of a climate functioning as a more or less stable support of vitality. In this sense, eco-anxiety fits the distinction Freud held onto for much of his work, although he would later abandon it, between realistic and neurotic types of anxiety.

Realistic anxiety relates to "particular external situations of danger" (SE 22: 93) and functions as a warning signal about a situation of danger (SE 20: 135), while neurotic anxiety replays either old and outdated dangers or equally old and outdated responses to such situations. With the Freudian distinction between types of anxiety, we thus return to Zabala's philosophy of warnings, nicely exemplified in the scientific study of catastrophic climate change and highlighting the existential threat it poses to human species and many other forms of life. Rather than a neurotic or a hysterical reaction, eco-anxiety is, on this view, an adaptive (or "expedient" as Freud qualifies realistic anxiety) mechanism, intended to send a signal about a future threat in order to flee from, fight, or adapt to that threat. This hyperrational explanation, in turn, obviates the need for a psychoanalytic intervention.

Yet, things are not as crystal clear as they may appear with respect to anxiety in general and eco-anxiety in particular. For one, anxiety is a reaction of the conscious ego, shaken by "a fear of death (or fear for life)," the reaction that is not shared by the unconscious: "the unconscious seems to contain nothing that could give any content to our concept of the annihilation of life" (SE 20: 129). In other words, the unconscious remains nonchalant in the face of mortal danger and impervious to all warning signs; in fact, it does not have an inkling of a future, which may be totally unlike the present. Conscious efforts will be subverted by the unconscious, with its demand of substitute satisfactions where these are not immediately provided.

A second look, with a side glance cast at the unconscious, examining the "fear of death" or anxiety against the background of the possibility of the loss of a livable world, will discover that this anxiety is like a false bottom drawer: there is another level lodged beneath the rational-adaptive apprehension. Freud notes that "the *affect* of anxiety" emanates from "the repressing agency itself," namely from the ego, and, moreover, that this anxiety is traceable to "the ego's fear of castration" (SE 20: 108–9). Mourned in advance, the loss of one's world is tantamount to losing something one never really possessed, never really controlled as an object; the world, eco-systems, a livable planet, a climate propitious to a biodiverse life—all these are the receiving, enveloping, diffuse structures that elude subjective mastery. The fear of castration in eco-anxiety, though, goes beyond these and is apprehensive about the loss of control (principally of technological mastery and domination) over what has never been either objectively controllable or reducible to an object. It may well be that the fear of death is not as primary as evolutionary theory makes us believe, but that it is a variation on the theme of control and its loss (here: control over the continuation of one's life or that of one's species). Death would be then understood as the most extreme instance of castration, of separation from one's entire body, rather than from a certain organ, taken to stand in a synecdochic relation to that body.

There are multiple threads in Freud's argument about anxiety that are tied in a single knot with the relation to technology and to the planetary body in the case of eco-anxiety. The enveloping, non-objectifiable nature of a climate or the world corresponds to the fetus's uterine environment prior to birth. In light of this correspondence, Freud's development of Otto Rank's thesis about the trauma of birth (at times in agreement with Rank; at other times rejecting his insights) is exceptionally relevant.

As late as 1932, in *New Introductory Lectures*, Freud affirms that birth is "our model for an anxiety state" (SE 22: 93). Like speculative ideation about death, probably also modeled on the event of birth, it is a wholesale separation of the child's body from the non-objectifiable, environment-like body of the mother and, hence, a prototype of extreme castration. Future instances of anxiety will replay the trauma of birth, along with the nascent mechanisms of repression that try to deal with that trauma: "The first and original repressions arise directly from traumatic moments, when the ego meets with an excessively great libidinal demand; they construct their anxiety afresh, although, it is true, on the model of birth" (SE 22: 94).

In its severity, the current environmental crisis alludes to the trauma of humanity's birth *as such*, its expulsion from the planetary-maternal body of the earth. Some celebrate the traumatic event as a possibility to establish human existence on other planets, for humanity to become an "interplanetary species." These attempts can hardly veil the anxiety of extreme separation from the earth and from the material conditions of possibility for life that the trauma portends.

To be sure, separation from the lifeworld has been a long-standing tendency of technologically savvy humanity, exaggerated especially in the phase of its industrialization. In contrast to the classical views on alienation, however, technology plays the double role of separation and of fulfilling the unconscious desire to be reunited with the world, from which one has been cut off. After all, technology is not only the prosthesis of human self-divinization, as Freud puts it in *Civilization and Its Discontents*, but also a phallic substitute, penetrating the planetary-maternal body so as to reunite with it after the event of birth.[3] This, for Freud, is the deepest sense of phallic symbols and their substitutes: the promise of reestablishing otherwise the original idyll of dwelling in a protective uterine environment.

Lest Freud's take on anxiety seem fanciful, its main point is a necessary supplement to all current considerations of eco-anxiety. Given the merging of conscious and unconscious provenances in this affect (conscious, because anxiety emanates from the ego itself; unconscious, because it replays responses to earlier situations of danger, perhaps going as far back as the "trauma of birth"), it is possible to say that two temporalities with their divergent orientations and outcomes intersect in the same affective state. The future-oriented temporality of a response to the impending danger is a warning sign, which may even function as a vaccine, an inoculation (SE 20: 162). "The signal announces: 'I am expecting a situation of helplessness to set in'" (SE 20: 166), and this announcement is performative: it visits upon the subject of the enunciation a sense of helplessness and trauma in a weakened and tacitly active way—that is its inoculation effect. By virtue of emitting anxiety affects and signals, "the ego, which experienced the trauma passively, now repeats it actively in a weakened version, in the hope of being able itself to direct its course" (SE 20: 167). The moment of repetition constitutes the past-oriented temporality of anxious response, which recalls previous situations of danger, again perhaps all the way back to the immemorial, from the standpoint of the one who is born, trauma of birth. Whereas the movement of repetition aims to take charge of what has been passively inflicted and to modify it by enacting it, the unconscious replay of past traumas ("as an automatic phenomenon," Freud observes [SE 20: 138]) merely brings back with it the sense of helplessness, resourcelessness, and abandonment associated with those past instances. The latter scenario is the one prevalent today both in the apocalyptic atmosphere of climate doom and in the hope-suffused techno-optimistic narratives about the rebirth of humanity as an interplanetary species that mask this overall helplessness.

In Freud's approach to anxiety, everything becomes double, from temporal orientations, to effects (expedient versus inexpedient), and from kinds of anxiety (realistic versus neurotic) to the psychical agencies that contribute to its emergence. The multiple "doublings" of anxiety in psychoanalysis are much more than simple bifurcations of its types; they are, rather, *speculative* doubles in the dialectical sense of the inclusion of X and not-X, a thing and its opposite, *in the same thing*.

The speculative doubling of anxiety applies to the paralysis it may give rise to. When anxiety is paralyzing, it obviously ceases to play a positive function: even if its danger signal is heeded, the stimulus is so overwhelming that one can no longer act upon it so as to thwart the impending threat. One facet of paralysis is attributable to a regressive return of helplessness, of "the infant's mental helplessness which is a natural counterpart of its biological helplessness" (SE 20: 138). Such a paralysis, due to a total lack of control and the incapacity to guarantee the satisfaction of instinctual need (SE 20: 139), is what we most commonly associate with the cases of eco-anxiety, where, beyond definite vital needs for shelter or nourishment, the entire sphere of habitability, livability, or vitality is affected. Freud supports this interpretation, but he also offers another, idiosyncratic one.

Paralysis in anxiety is the extreme case of inhibition, of "a *restriction of an ego-function*," which comes to interfere with the functioning of specific organs (SE 20: 89). Freud suggests that this fate befalls organs that are excessively eroticized: "the ego-function of an organ is impaired if its erotogenicity—its sexual significance—is increased" (SE 20: 89). Before the differentiation of the ego, the erotogenicity of the entire body of the infant—polymorphous perversity—may be seen as an expression of the inhibited functionality of its organs due to their heightened sexual significance. (This hypothesis accords with plant processes, in which sexual efflorescence stops vegetative growth—that is, the "normal" behavior of plants and the expected functionality of their organs.) In the situation of eco-anxiety, a paralyzing feeling could be attributed to the sexualization of either our extended planetary-climatic body or our relation to the body of the earth. Freud undersigns the latter interpretative option in an example he gives of an anxiety-induced erotogenic paralysis: "As soon as writing, which entails making a liquid flow of a tube on to a piece of white paper, assumes the significance of copulation, or as soon as walking becomes a symbolic substitute for treading upon the body of mother earth, both writing and walking are stopped because they represent the performance of a forbidden sexual act" (SE 20: 90).

Whatever its source, the paralyzing effect of anxiety—including, of course, eco-anxiety—is not adaptive, not expedient, to the extent to which it prevents preparations for a future where the existential danger, signaled by anxiety, materializes. Then, a sense of doom, of the end of days, of resignation before the inevitability of extinction prevails. But inexpedient anxious responses need not be so blatant. Given the temporal mismatch between the earliest anxious states, going back to the very beginning of a person's life, and the present or future situation of endangerment, another mismatch creeps into the psychological situation—the mismatch between a recalled (or a phantasmatically returning) anxiety and the means for dealing with the more recently generated problems. Hence, Freud: "When the anxiety-state is reproduced later as an affect it will be lacking any [. . .] expediency, just as are the repetitions of a hysterical attack. When the individual is placed in a new situation of danger it may well be quite inexpedient for him to respond with an anxiety-state (which is a reaction to an earlier danger) instead of initiating a reaction appropriate to the current danger" (SE 20: 134).

Isn't this precisely what happens with regard to anxious responses to the climate crisis on a scale that by far exceeds individual reactions? While technological development in an effort to "dominate" and "tame" the unruly external nature was, at an earlier point in human history, a compensation for castration anxiety, the same strategy is bound to be inexpedient in dealing with the fallout from the technogenic deregulation of climates, ecosystems, and so forth. The means to tackle anxiety-inducing occurrences will spawn further anxiety, sharpening the knife or the guillotine. Activist and environmentalist discourses of "climate debt," as of any other debt that is ultimately unpayable, and the attendant financialization of the struggle against catastrophic climate change lend a material (monetary) expression to this snowballing of anxiety, itself mirroring the dynamics of capital.

For its part, anxiety avoidance, which causes more harm than good, is the compensatory logic verging on a compulsion. Freud discusses the effects of anxiety on the nutritive function, with regard to two possible disturbances: the disinclination to eat and overeating. Concerning the latter, he writes: "An increase in the desire to eat is also a not uncommon thing. The compulsion to eat is attributed to a fear of starving; but this is a subject which has been but little studied" (SE 20: 88). The fear of energy starvation, of running out of the "natural resources" that can be burnt as fossil sources of fuel, feeds the compulsion to consume ever-increasing amounts of energy, or to accumulate it. The very category of "renewables" is a symptom of this insatiable compulsion, rejecting any external checks and balances on capital's (rather than human) need and desire for unlimited energy. It is this nutritive anxiety of capitalist machinery that makes huge inroads in swaying individuals and governments toward the nuclear energy option, with the underside of a dangerous and unmanageable drive to accumulation, namely the accumulation of spent nuclear materials that cannot be either safely stored or deactivated.

That the chain of substitutions in anxiety (where anxious ideation substitutes for a deeper, repressed source of unpleasure) is so long as to be virtually endless is attributable to the connection of this affect to the earliest (pre-) experiences, pointing all the way back to birth. "The ideas contained in anxiety [. . .] were substitutes by distortion for the idea of being castrated [. . .]" (SE 20: 108). This means that we need to seek, below the surface of consciously identified motivations for the currently widespread eco-anxiety, other—often anachronistic—reasons. Anxiety in the face of climate breakdown and eco-systems' collapse is the distorted substitute for the fear of death (individual and that of the species), which is itself a substitute for the fear of castration, which, finally or in the first instance, stands in for the primal fear of separation.

Curiously, in the case of eco-anxiety, the chain of substitutions does not result in the image of infinite regress, which comes through in Freud's analysis of the theme. The anxiety implicit in the presentiment of separation from and loss of something or someone that is not an object—something or someone enveloping one's body-mind and gifting one with the possibilities of life, breath, and nourishment—returns in the fear of being removed from a climate and an environment propitious to the maintenance of individual and species vitality. It closes the circle in a mode of the infinite that is distinct from that of a straight line tending to infinity and replays at the level of conscious and unconscious grasp what could not yet constitute an experience in the anxiety of birth.

For his part, Freud sees in primal anxiety a marker of primary narcissism (which will also be the root of the instinct of self-preservation): "birth is not experienced subjectively as a separation from the mother, since the fetus, being a completely narcissistic creature, is totally unaware of her existence as an object" (SE 20: 130). The question is not only whether in the environmental crisis something of this separation is experienced subjectively or not, retrospectively illuminating the event of birth as the event of *naturing*, but also whether at the wobbly edges of separation, which is not felt as such, the ego is born with or from anxiety, so that there would be no ego without anxiety. If the latter holds true, then the ego is, more than "the actual seat of anxiety" (SE 20: 93), its actual offshoot, with the arrow of causality between the two inverted (Freud argues that "the ego [is] the source of anxiety" [SE 20: 161], whereas it is anxiety that is the source of the ego). Eco-anxiety is an acute case of ego-anxiety in this sense: it testifies to the possibility of a birth of humanity's planetary ego, with all the positive and negative implications of such a momentous occasion, which is nonetheless inseparable from the planetary unconscious.

B

Biodiversity conundrums (with an eye to the death drive)

Biodiversity, its cherishing and protection, is one of those values that is taken to be beyond reproach and is totally immune to critique. Around such "untouchable" issues, we should be able to detect the highest degrees of repression, making a negative approach all but unthinkable—literally, not reaching the threshold of consciousness, of what may be thought. So, what are those traces of negativity in the concept of biodiversity?

Once the first line of defense is surmounted, the issue becomes embarrassingly conspicuous: biodiversity is too abstract of a concept to account for life, for its vibrancy and fine-grained textures, for the tensions and frictions that permeate its fabric and make it what it is. Life (*bios*) splinters into an indifferent manifold (diversity) of forms; the difference at the heart of biodiversity is an indifferent difference, neutral and neutralizing, oblivious to its content. And this takes us directly to Freud's reflections on life and death instincts both in *Beyond the Pleasure Principle* and in *The Ego and the Id*.

Before discussing the relation of biodiversity to life and death instincts, a note on intellectualization is in order. In *The Ego and the Id*, Freud puts forth what he admits to be a hypothesis. "It seems a plausible view," he writes there, "that this displaceable and neutral energy, which is no doubt active both in the ego and in the id, proceeds from the narcissistic store of libido—that it is desexualized Eros" (SE 19: 44). Freud further highlights "a certain indifference as to the path along which the discharge takes place," translating into "a peculiar indifference in regard to the object" (SE 19: 45). He then speculates on this sort of neutral and indifferent energy as the source of thinking: "If thought-processes in the wider sense are to be included among these displacements, then the activity of thinking is also supplied from the sublimation of erotic motive forces" (SE 19: 45).

Just about *any* abstraction could be understood as the neutral and indifferent product of displaced and desexualized libidinal energy, but the abstraction of biodiversity occupies a place of its own. Here, it is life (*bios*) that is reduced to the indifferent difference of diverse forms and, therefore, remolded in the image of death. The intellectualization that yields this concept is quantifiable (biodiversity as a living manifold) and analytic (diversity not amounting to synthetic agglomeration). It militates not so much against the category of quality as against the content of life, which is the ever-renewed tension with other lives and with death. The placement of all forms of life on the same plane of diversity is a radical egalitarian move, and, by the same stroke, a move that undercuts the vitality of life itself, rendering it docile, manipulable, administrable, and, ultimately, moribund. Abstract equality, after all, veers very close to death; opposition to the organization of differences, as well as of difference and sameness, in hierarchies does not necessarily imply a total flattening, as in "flat ontology" or "deep ecology," where everything is equivalent to everything else. Freud notes that "death is an abstract concept with a negative content, for which no unconscious correlative can be found" (SE 19: 58), and his characterization applies, *mutatis mutandis*, to pure equality and biodiversity.

Recapping his theory of instincts in the 1938 *Outline of Psychoanalysis*, Freud revisits the relation between "Eros (or the love instinct)" and "the destructive instinct," the final aim of which "is to lead what is living into an inorganic state" (SE 23: 148–9). Under the sway of neutralization, cast in intellectual terms, these tendencies are synthesis and analysis, but in practical terms, the "concurrent and mutually opposing action of the two basic instincts gives rise to the whole variegation of the phenomena of life" (SE 23: 149). Now, this description contrasts sharply with the insipid idea of biodiversity: "the whole variegation of the phenomena of life" is not an indifferent manifold of biodiversity, but the dynamic outcome of life and death instincts, working in tandem and in opposition to each other. Evolutionary development and the involution of organic forms returning to the inorganic state are the driving forces behind the "variegation" of life.

Freud formulates the actions of the two instincts in *Beyond the Pleasure Principle* (1920), where evolutionary and involutionary trajectories sweep through organic life and build up the psychological-instinctive force pertaining to this life. The increasing complexity of evolution is counterbalanced by involution, with the "final goal of all organic striving" being death (SE 18: 38). The emanation of life from its inorganic other is coupled with the "instinct to return to the inanimate state" (SE 18: 38). Just as the lines of egress from the inorganic realm are more and more complex, so the backward-pointing paths are more difficult to follow—an organism "makes ever more complicated *détours* before reaching its aim of death" (SE 18: 39). The loss of biodiversity attributable to anthropogenic factors is a pure case of the death instinct, not only leading a vast number of species to their demise but also aiming to reduce much of organic existence to the inorganic state. Nevertheless, the negativity of "loss" is something of a tautology when it comes to biodiversity; as we have already seen, the transformation of life (*bios*) under the influence of diversity already contains the seeds of the death instinct sublimated into an abstract treatment of vitality.

The theory of the death instinct, first formulated by Sabina Spielrein in a 1912 paper, "Destruction as the Cause of Coming into Being,"[1] is a rejoinder to the theoretical position, according to which the instinct of self-preservation is the one universal drive in all living beings, obeying the injunction of primary narcissism. It renders all positive philosophies of immanence and positivisms implausible. In Freud's view, the function of the death instinct is "to assure that the organism shall follow its own path to death, and to ward off any possible ways of returning to inorganic existence other than those which are immanent to the organism itself" (SE 18: 39). In other words, in facing mortal threats, organisms do not oppose death per se, but, rather, the possibility of dying in a way that is inappropriate to their kind of existence. This line of thinking precedes by eight years Heidegger's reflections in *The Fundamental Concepts of Metaphysics* (1928) on perishing, demise, and "authentic" death, indexed to human and other-than-human beings. But how exactly does a drastic reduction in biodiversity fit the paradigm of the death instinct?

On the one hand, this loss in the trail of the sixth mass extinction imposes a uniform possibility and actuality of dying on miscellaneous kinds of existence. It amounts to the acceleration and simplification of paths to death that are different lives; instead of "complicated *détours*," the same fate awaits all, or nearly all, in an ever more direct route to the demise of species and the organisms who comprise them. On the other hand, and at the same time, anthropogenic and technogenic mass extinction imposes a particular industrialized reality of death onto the world of the living; it is a historically and culturally specific human way of "returning to inorganic existence" generalized and extended to other species. That is, the death instinct of the industrializing and industrialized humanity, while proper to it, *does not assure* the normal functioning of the same instinct in non-human animals and plants, fungi and bacteria. It is indifferent to the different and oft-incomparable paths various kinds of organisms take to their end.

Freud further speculates that the renewal of life is due to "the influx of fresh amounts of stimulus," notably in the shape of "union with the living substance of a different individual [which] increases those tensions, introducing what may be described as fresh 'vital differences'" (SE 18: 55). The reduction of tensions and "vital differences" is, conversely, an offshoot of the death instinct, expressed in biodiversity loss. In and of itself, biodiversity is not a gathering of "vital differences," but indifferent difference, void of enlivening tensions, and, as such, anticipating (if not harboring in its very formative conception) the death instinct, which is perversely actualized on an unprecedented scale. It is, to reiterate, a managerial term, attached to life already neutralized, readied for administration and manipulation, deprived of meaningful differences, and already dead before mass extinction has set in.

The standard response to biodiversity loss is conservationism, and it, too, is liable to a psychoanalytic reading. In fact, both basic instincts are conservative. Sexual instincts "are conservative in the same sense as the other [death] instincts in that they bring back earlier states of living substance; but they are conservative to a higher degree in that they are peculiarly resistant to external influences; and they are conservative too in another sense in that they preserve life itself for a comparatively long period" (SE 18: 40).

The first sense of "conservative" is applicable to life and death instincts: the former reduce an organism to the genetic code and its carriers, restarting life from the beginning (e.g., conception, embryonic development that recaptures in a miniature and in a condensed time period the development of a species, if not of the history of life itself, etc.), while the latter harken back to the inorganic state, from which organic life emerged. Paradoxically, the ultimate goal of death instincts is not destruction but conservation: of matter in its inorganic state, which promises more substantive stability than organic matter. Conservatism and conservationism boil down to reductionism—not to care about actual living beings but about their inorganic museumization or about the possibility of their genetic code being clothed with flesh again in the future, if and when the need arises. This logic impels the creation of seed or germplasm banks, among other biorepositories, that contravene *and* reinforce biodiversity loss in its essentially conservative aspect.

The second sense of the "conservative" nature of instincts applies exclusively to life instincts that resist external influences—for example, those no longer propitious to the ongoing growth, flourishing, or future existence of any given living being. The idea is that, as much as possible, organismic homeostasis is maintained in the face of an assault from external environment. However, as Freud does not tire to mention, the "homeostasis" of the living is vital difference and a state of tension constitutive of and invigorating life. It is, then, a case of counterbalancing the psycho-physiological tension of life with the pressures, including those of the most threatening kind, from external factors. And that is not even to mention the inner threats to ongoing organismic existence, threats that derive from the byproducts of the body's metabolic life-processes (SE 18: 46). What kills us is nothing other than life, but each sort of life kills in its own way. Here, "conservative" really means "revolutionary": the sense of conservation is inverted on its own terms into resistance, adaptation, and so forth. Conservationism, as well, is a tool for opposing adverse external influences, if at the price of idealization, the preservation of ecosystems and species that is tantamount to freezing them in time. Such an opposition approximates the dissolution of tensions and the absolute rest of inorganic substances (or of Platonic ideas).

The third sense of "conservative" life instincts dovetails with the second and implies the preservation of life "for a comparatively long period." The relative and conditional nature of this formulation elucidates the differences between life and death instincts in view of the possibilities of their satisfaction. A complete dissolution of tension and, consequently, a total satisfaction of the striving to return to the inorganic state is only conceivable in the case of death instinct (allied with the absolute and the ideal or the idealizable), whereas for a life instinct "the backward path that leads to complete satisfaction is as a rule obstructed by the resistances which maintain the repressions. So there is no alternative but to advance in the direction in which growth is still free" (SE 18: 42). The objective of conservationism is to extend, to make comparatively longer, the period of life's preservation, but, if it veers toward life instincts, then its striving is bound to be frustrated. The maintenance of vital differences must nourish their inner tensions, rather than stabilize or conserve the molds of organisms and ecosystems, which are but moments in the dynamic unfolding and enfolding of life at a "vacillating rhythm" (SE 18: 41). A vibrant conservationism is, of necessity, revolutionary: its object is not biodiversity but the multiple tensions of life and the living, of life and death instincts, and of the mutually opposed senses of conservatism (preserving life and retreating to an older inorganic state).

Neither the practices and attitudes that are prejudicial to biodiversity nor the concept of biodiversity itself grasp "the compulsion to repeat" guiding every stirring of instinct (SE 18: 36–7). Ultimately, Freud implies, all instincts have the shape of an ellipse, in which the ascending and descending nodes—the phases of evolution and involution, of development and regress—coalesce. The destruction of biodiversity singles out the involutive, descending trajectory; the fetishization of biodiversity privileges the ascending and evolutive curves. But, insofar as the notion of biodiversity neutralizes living differences, its partisans acquiesce with the death instinct, smuggled through the backdoor, so to speak. Freud concludes that life is more than life, dialectically structured as it is by a struggle with death: "Our speculations have suggested that Eros operates from the beginning of life and appears as a 'life instinct' in opposition to the 'death instinct' which was brought into being by the coming to life of inorganic substance" (SE 18: 61). With biodiversity, which at best obscures the unificatory operations of the life instinct and at worst infringes upon them, the terms are inverted: death is produced as death in an internal opposition to life, just because the movement of extinction is temporally and logically dependent on the existence of organic substance.

Casting a retrospective glance at his theory of instincts in *The Ego and the Id*, Freud emphasizes a decisive step in the "neutralization" of death instinct: "It appears that, as a result of the combination of unicellular organisms into multicellular forms of life, the death instinct of a single cell can be successfully neutralized and the destructive impulses be diverted on to the external world through the instrumentality of a special organ" (SE 23: 41). In contemporary microbiology, even a single cell is considered a symbiotic assemblage of its organelles—an alliance that is later on reaffirmed at the level of a multicellular organism. By implication, much rides on the construal of biodiversity as a combination or a splintering of forms of life and, therefore, as a concept in the service of death or life instincts. If biodiversity is an ever particularizing, singularizing phenomenon, then it inherently contains destructive impulses, anticipating death. (In social and economic, as well as political and ontological terms, privatization plays a similar role.) If it is a combinatory force, mappable onto a "tree of life," then it is under the aegis of the life instinct, though the next question concerns the kinds of differences and the *how* of their combination in biodiverse existence. Ontologically and axiologically neutral and indifferent differences retain the pull of the death instinct even if, ostensibly, they are harnessed for the sake of life. This is the conundrum of biodiversity, spanning life and death instincts, gains and losses, productive and destructive conservatism.

To circle back to the beginning of our reflection on biodiversity as a relatively recent intellectualization of the concept of life with a strong managerial bent, it is worth asking how to interpret reactions to its *loss*. There is a significant gap between the experiential dimension of no longer spotting particular species of plants or animals, such as bees and butterflies who used to frequent a certain meadow in previous years, and the intellectual plane, on which the diminution and loss of biodiversity make sense. Needless to say, the two levels are linked, but decrying biodiversity loss may water down the experiential and affective components of missing an encounter with the now extinct or disappearing plants and animals. In the absence of an encounter, what is prominent is *a failure of repetition*, the displeasure felt (as a symptom of the frustrated instinct) when, unlike in previous years, these inter-species encounters do not come to pass. (Encounters may be thought of as fleeting combinations, favorable to the life instinct, which, for Freud, is a manifestation of "the sexual instincts" rather than of "the ego-instincts" [SE 18: 44].) In keeping with the dynamics of intellectualization, biodiversity loss is marked, in Freud's words, by "a peculiar indifference in regard to the object." The intensity of affect (e.g., of sorrow) will be greatly diminished in this case, seeing that it will be an affect attached to a displaced and sublimated object.

It follows that the conundrums of biodiversity cannot be resolved, and least of all can they be resolved by intellectual means. A systematic reconstruction of ecological experiences, practices, discourses, and theories is required to move past them.

C

Civilization and its (presumed) anti-ecologism

Since the third decade of the twenty-first century, some groups of eco-activists (such as Just Stop Oil, Extinction Rebellion, Riposte Alimentaire, or The Last Generation) took in rather big numbers to a symbolic and not-so-symbolic public destruction of works of art in order to draw attention to insufficient measures taken in the global fight against catastrophic global heating and climate change. The rationale behind these démarches is that, for public opinion and its average sensibilities, it is much more shocking that an artwork is threatened with destruction than the actual devastation of ecosystems or global climate havoc. What is interrogated by protest actions taking place in (predominantly European) art galleries and museums is the topsy-turvy reality, where art is worth more than life (or ecology), where cultural products are cherished and preserved, while countless human and other-than-human lives are condemned to perishing. Protestors, in their turn, accept and intensify the standoff between civilization and nature, or between the treatment of cultural and natural heritages, shedding light onto the real destruction of life via a symbolic destruction of prized artefacts.

In the opening pages of *The Future of an Illusion*, Freud argues that "art offers substitutive satisfaction for the still most deeply felt cultural renunciations, and for that reason it serves as nothing else does to reconcile a man to the sacrifices he has made on behalf of civilization" (SE 21: 14). Freud adds that "as a rule, it [i.e., art] remains inaccessible to the masses, who are engaged in exhausting work and have not enjoyed any personal education"

(SE 21: 13). To eco-activists, works of art are accessible, in many senses of the term, but, in their unconscious calculus, renunciation is not compensated for by the substitute satisfactions of art. One could say that, here, in addition to the renunciation of instinct and of its immediate satisfaction, there is a realization that civilization demands the repudiation of a livable world, tipping the scales against the most widely recognizable instances of sublimation that represent civilization in a nutshell. The destructive force of civilization then boomerangs against that same civilization via the crumbling of its life supports.

Writing in 1927, Freud notes that those who do not identify with a civilization "are not prepared to acknowledge the prohibitions, they are intent on destroying the culture itself, and possibly even on doing away with the postulates on which it is based" (SE 21: 12). Eco-activists who, nearly one hundred years later, attack prominent artworks in museums go only halfway in acting upon such an intent: they engage in symbolic acts of destruction against symbolic artefacts, most often knowing that they will cause no lasting or permanent damage. In a similar vein, elaborate acknowledgments of indigenous land claims, with which many intellectual contributions (whether oral or written) are prefaced, do not budge from the symbolic domain, in that they are not followed by a real restitution of lands, territories, and sovereignty to indigenous groups. Disavowals of cultural renunciation and of the renunciation of this renunciation leave the impression that they are part of an ever more elaborate game of simultaneously holding onto *and* negating the oppressive legacies of colonialism and capitalism, of genocidal history and environmental devastation. Nevertheless, going all the way to a violent destruction of cultural heritage would tacitly undersign the ongoing violence, whether slow or fast, that is decimating the natural heritage of the planet: ecosystems, species, and elemental domains.

Freud lists two main means and goals of civilization: "it includes on the one hand all the knowledge and capacity that men have acquired in order to control the forces of nature and extract its wealth for the satisfaction of human needs, and, on the other hand, all the regulations necessary in order to adjust the relations of men to one another and especially the distribution of the available wealth" (SE 21: 6). The Freudian distinction repeats the traditional Jewish interpretation of the ten commandments, with the first five said to regulate the human relation to God and the last five to dictate the norms of inter-human relations, except that in Freud's text, which treats religion as an illusion, instead of God we find nature (as we do, also, in Spinoza's *Ethics*). That said, there is nothing ethical about the forces of civilization bearing down upon nature, which is subject to control and extraction. On Freud's reading, civilization as such (rather than Western civilization per se) is anti-ecological. More than that, if "every civilization must be built up on coercion and renunciation of instinct" (SE 21: 7), then its part adjudicating inter-human relations appears to be a strict corollary to the control and extractivism characteristic of its approach to the other-than-human world. Civilization posits itself against external nature as much as against the mix of human, animal, vegetal, and even mineral components of human existence. It requires the renunciation of instinct, "detach[ing] man from his primordial animal condition" (SE 21: 10).

Since there are two basic instincts—life and death—the demand of civilization is also double. Critical theorists of the Frankfurt school (above all, Herbert Marcuse) examined in excruciating detail the process and consequences of "surplus repression," associated with the renunciation of the life instinct. But a benighted hypercivilized human being does not have the luxury of cultivating the death instinct either; the conservative vector of the compulsion to repeat, to return to the inorganic condition or any other earlier stages of life's development, is foreclosed. The ideology of progress, for example, does not pay attention to death (a problem that philosophers from Kant and Hegel to Dostoyevsky and Fedorov tried to solve, in very different ways); perhaps, it is as unaware of death as the unconscious, albeit for another reason altogether. At its "advanced" stage, civilization thus reaches an impasse, disallowing both living and dying.

The exceptionally close ties between the extractive-dominating thrust of civilization and its repressive-renunciative effects are evident in Freud's thought. That is why, for him, a non-extractive and non-repressive civilization is simply unimaginable, though neither propensity can accomplish its goal entirely. With every newborn and with every new generation, "instinctual wishes" are also reborn, as strong as ever (SE 21: 10).

With regard to non-human nature, Freud admits that full control over it is illusory, adding another twist to his treatise on "the future of an illusion": "There are the elements, which seem to mock all human control: the earth, which quakes and is torn apart and buries human life and its works; water, which deluges and drowns everything in a turmoil; storms, which blow everything before them; there are diseases, which we have only recently recognized as attacks by other organisms; and finally there is the painful riddle of death, against which no medicine has yet been found, nor probably will be. With these forces, nature rises up against us, majestic, cruel and inexorable" (SE 21: 15–16). Concentrating on the purely uncontrollable, untamable excess of nature, Freud does not entertain the possibility that another, more insidious kind of uncontrollability arises as a function of increased control, first and foremost, the control inherent to the two founding tasks of civilization. This is precisely what happens with the climate mayhem, which is a technogenic upshot of the exploitation of nature. It would not be a big stretch of the imagination to assert, analogously, that unprecedented unconscious deregulation results from the strictest degree of self-control, repression, and renunciation of instinct.

Regardless of its root causes, the overwhelming, uncontrollable power of nature (in the garb of Fate) deals a severe blow to human narcissism (SE 21: 16). Instead of working through wounded narcissism, the average response is "outsourcing" further transactions with nature to civilization, now as an affective-ideational-ideological bandage, covering the wound. Freud cites "the humanization of nature" among such strategies (SE 21: 16). Currently, studies on the intelligence of other-than-human beings, including plants, are accused of humanizing these beings, of projecting an anthropomorphic ideal onto them. The accusations miss the mark: intelligence is not the prerogative of *Homo sapiens* but a feature of all life forms, adapted to their unique modes of being. At their most radical, inquiries into vegetal, animal, fungal, bacterial, or ecosystem intelligences do not take part in the civilizational project of humanization; in fact, one of their side effects, shared with Freud's notion of the unconscious, is the *de*humanization of the human. The next frontier would be shifting the focus from the intentionality and decision-making capacities of other-than-human organisms to vegetal, animal, fungal, bacterial, and ecosystem *unconscious*.

Thinking like a mountain is unthinkable without dreaming and desiring like a mountain: a civilization where ideas like these will not seem odd will no longer be essentially anti-ecological, and psychoanalysis will play no small part in this transformation.

The humanization of nature is a cog in the apparatus of religion, which takes over the mission of civilization ("the necessity of defending oneself against the crushingly superior force of nature"), while also responding to "the urge to rectify the shortcomings of civilization" (SE 21: 21). As a result, religious ideas deepen the anti-ecological stance as Freud conceives of it *and* they bridge the growing chasm between the civilized world and nature. The competing ideologies of transcendence and immanence are reconciled on the grounds of religious meta-ecumenicalism. There is, consequently, a grain of (psychoanalytic) truth in portrayals of ecological thought as a new religion: it does "urge to rectify the shortcomings of civilization" by renouncing extraction and control as the principal rules of engagement with non-human nature, but it also responds to the "necessity of defending oneself" against nature's "crushingly superior force," now mediated and amplified by the byproducts of industrial mass pollution.

What changes is that, if ecological thought is a religion, it is a religion without the threatening-protective father figure. That is probably why the ecological defense is no longer standoffish; it takes the side of the "superior force" and claims this force for itself, as its own (albeit non-appropriable) potentiality. Rather than capitulation, it is a stratagem of influencing non-human nature without mastery, an avowed weakness acclaimed as a higher strength. So, too, the humanization of nature among other religious phenomena is, for Freud, "derived from the need to put an end to man's perplexity and helplessness in the face of its dreaded forces, to get into a relation with them and finally to influence them" (SE 21: 22).

A civilization that is not anti-ecological is possible, even in the post-industrial West. Freud calls a hopeless approach to helplessness "an infantile model" (SE 21: 22), in which "the growing individual finds that he is destined to remain a child for ever" (SE 21: 24). That said, the knowledge of one's limitations and dependence on others, be they human or not, is more mature than the Enlightenment ideal of perfect autonomy, particularly provided that the ecological position of dependence is not projected onto and accepted vis-à-vis the divine Other. It is an infantilism that is wiser than the serious philosophical stance, to which "self-incurred immaturity" is abhorrent. And one of the implications of this thesis is that the ecological position (at least in one of its incarnations) is polymorphously perverse, in line with infantile sexuality. Polymorphous perversity is not confined to the individual body of an eco-subject and its different erotogenic zones but extends to the world at large, the body of the world and everyone inhabiting it. Genital sexuality and the reproductive function cease to be the teleological molds (imposed by a repressive, anti-ecological civilization) for sexuality as such, releasing child play back to itself and to its planetary environs.

But, though possible, such a civilization is far from actual. In addition to the increasing dissatisfaction with and unhappiness in civilization, which Freud diagnoses in "an appallingly large number of people" (SE 21: 37), the awareness that the clash of civilization with inner nature (instinct) and with outer nature is suicidal and lethal for the biosphere is also growing. This feeling no longer conforms to the moderate unease, discomfort, disquiet, or even discontent (*Unbehagen*), which Freud attributes to civilization in the title of his other major treatise on it—the discontent *with* civilization, to be sure, but also the discontent *of* civilization, one that is of a piece with it. The technological prostheses that are the achievements of contemporary culture hurt more than they assist the body of humanity wearing them and the planetary body bearing them. Freud's judgment on how the "auxiliary" or "prosthetic" techno-organs of humanity "have not grown on to him [on to man, MM] and they still give him much trouble at times" (SE 21: 92) now sounds too lenient. The "actual fulfilment of every—or of almost every—fairy-tale wish" (SE 21: 91) thanks to technological innovation has turned into the nightmare of mass suffocation, poisoning, toxicity, heat exhaustion, and the like. As in individual psychic life, civilizational wish fulfillment exacts a steep price: while the subject's immediate satisfaction of instinct leads to social opprobrium and legal punishments, a comparable satisfaction at the level of the entire civilization entails ecological reprimands and retributions. The reality principle not only keeps wish fulfillment in check but also converts realized dreams into the worst nightmares, not least those of the ecological kind.

Freud counts philosophy and art, as well as religion, among the "higher mental activities" esteemed by civilization, in light of "the leading role it assigns to ideas in human life" (SE 21: 94). For these ideas not to be either vacuous or harmful (when implemented) ideals, it is necessary for them to act as living membranes between civilization and the lived environment, reconnecting with our animal, vegetal, and inorganic ancestry, in contrast to the civilization, which Freud defines as "the whole sum of achievements and regulations which distinguish our lives from those of our animal ancestors" (SE 21: 89). Unless a practical redefinition of civilization is attempted along these lines, no longer opposing the overwhelming forces of nature and other-than-human forms of life—that is to say, unless civilization moves past its anti-ecological stance—it will continue on the path of self-destruction, which Freud had already intuited, and of the destruction of vast portions of a livable world.

This would not be inconsistent with Freud's own projection: "And now, I think, the meaning of the evolution of civilization is no longer obscure to us. It must present the struggle between Eros and Death, between the instinct of life and the instinct of destruction, as it works itself out in the human species" (SE 21: 122). In the twenty-first century, the evolution he invokes tends to an involution: "the instinct of destruction" seems to be gaining the upper hand, no longer locked in a struggle with the life instinct, but remolding life and death alike. More than any other approach, psychoanalysis is capable of elucidating the deep, unconscious roots of this predicament and integrating environmental activism with the much-needed self-analysis of activist desires, feeding into programs and actions.

D

Dump, defecation

In *Dump Philosophy*, I suggested an interpretation of the Anthropocene as the planetary dump of the techno-body that strews non-decomposable or barely decomposable materials and byproducts of industrial production across all ecosystems, elemental domains, and even the cosmic vicinities of the earth. There, I revisited Freud's take on defecation, according to which children view their feces as parts of their bodies, as a sacrificial gift to the world, and finally as their own progeny.[1] That work served as preparation for a psychoanalytic understanding of the clogged ecosystems, of "forever chemicals" released into the environment, of plastics and nuclear waste, as well as of Big Data, light or sound pollution, static metaphysical ideas, and so forth. Those initial insights need to be further honed both within a wider range of Freud's texts and with respect to the contradictions that immanently structure the epoch of the dump with its anal fixations.

In some of the earliest associations of character traits with anal erotism, Freud highlights the qualities of being "*orderly* [ordentlich], *parsimonious* and *obstinate*" (SE 9: 169). Predating this 1908 essay are Freud's epistolary reflections on the relation between miserliness with feces retention in an 1897 letter to Fliess and analogous insights shared with Jung in a letter that dates back to 1906. All of these character traits are traceable to the refusal to empty one's bowels, a withholding of the feces with the view to deriving "a subsidiary pleasure from defecating" after a period of its delay or deferral (SE 9: 170). When these qualities are transposed onto the overall state of being, which I have termed "dump" and which becomes ontologically prominent in the twenty-first century, the first immanent contradiction becomes apparent. The gargantuan volumes of pollution dumped into the atmosphere, the oceans, social or political space of coexistence, or online are neither withheld nor let go of; instead, their letting-go-of *is* their withholding, their release triggering the indigestion of non-decomposable, non-processable, impassible materials, information, or ideas. As a result, the moment of deriving accumulated pleasure from the release of these scatological byproducts of the techno- or civilizational body is infinitely deferred *and* it is immediate, unending insofar as the uninterrupted outpouring of what is dumped is concerned.

The obstinacy of the dumped, its resistance to metabolism and to the effects of time itself, is evident. Less so are orderliness and parsimoniousness: the dump is, by definition, disorderly (a haphazard mix of heterogenous, fragmented materials) and in its massiveness it is anything but moderate. Nevertheless, the same structural contradiction is inherent in capitalism: despite the primary and the ongoing accumulation, the logic of capital requires its equally ongoing and ever-growing release into the cycles of reinvestment. Before it is transformed into one, the world from the standpoint of capital is already a dump, in that (as far as use-value is concerned) it is a matter of pure non-differentiation and indifference as to which commodities are being produced. And, for an individual capitalist, it only makes sense to reinvest capital along with the profits it yields, rather than squander it. Capitalist pleasure is infinitely deferred *and* it is perversely unending: at any rate, it is not the material pleasure related to use, however luxurious the usable items, but the pleasure derived from the process of accumulation and reinvestment, anal withholding and massive release of capital.

The above line of thought holds for "natural capital," as well: its accumulation is not a value in itself, nor even, as the rationalizations of this term make it appear, a precondition for current or future use. Natural capital is perfectly appropriate to the anal-defecatory-dumped conception of nature in the world, or in the unworld, of the dump. Orderly scientific classificatory systems coincide here with the saturation of all organisms and ecosystems with industrial byproducts, such as micro- and nanoplastics. The obstinate refusal to let species go, expressed in the conservationist impulse, matches on its obverse the non-decomposable elements, with which the biosphere is laced and which would not go away. The parsimonious decision not to waste natural capital belongs together with the quantification of all that lives, the assignment of economic value, and a potential or actual wholesale investment of dumped nature into the production process.

As I noted in *Dump Philosophy*, the attitudes of finding the dump reality of the Anthropocene disgusting and taking pleasure in it are two sides of the same coin. Freud observes that "reaction-formations, or counter-forces, such as shame, disgust, and morality" are "actually formed at the expense of the excitations proceeding from the erotogenic zones" (SE 9: 171). The forces and counter-forces of expression and repression (that, in their interactions, form symptoms, those twisted and indirect expressions shaped by repressive mechanisms) correspond to the released and the withheld, whether at the affective or at the substantive level. The disgusted pride awakened by the Anthropocene, symptomatically apparent already in the scientific naming of this geological epoch, is a reflection of the excremental-dumped massive release *and* the withholding of the stuff that lends the Anthropocene its identity. The Anthropocene is the anal phase of humanity, which recognizes itself in and transfigures the entire planet into shit, albeit not into manure, which could enrich the soil for the growth to come, but into non-decomposable remains. In the same way, the affective discharge mixing disgust with secret pride in this achievement does not admit further development; it is stuck, it is stuckness itself.

Where Freud was convinced that the character traits he analyzed were "the sublimation of anal erotism" (SE 9: 171), in the world of the Anthropocene no such sublimation is possible. The tendency, which, in the middle of the past century, Marcuse labeled "repressive de-sublimation," referring to the regressive return of sublimated works to the sphere of sexuality without lifting repression, becomes more extreme. If the qualities of orderliness, miserliness, and obstinacy are the sublimations of anal erotism, their de-sublimation harkens back to the source, to that which was to be sublimated. In this movement, the disorder of non-differentiation, the immense outpouring, and the staying power of the dump are mixed with reaction formations, such as the emphasis on "clean energy" (its polluting effects often merely hidden from view or displaced). Rather than internally overcome the problem of pollution, the discursive construction of *clean energy* is a sign of its repression and de-sublimation; it is "a reaction-formation against an interest in what is unclean and disturbing and should not be part of the body" (SE 9: 172). In their general framing, these and related solutions resemble "complexes of interest" (SE 9: 173), or fixations that gather a vast network of cathexes and entire semantic fields around themselves. What is required is the exact opposite: not complexifying further the civilizational character type and its relation to ecology, but working through, disentangling the complex, pursuing the work of analysis, painful or absurd as it may feel.

That is where the notion of the dump and its excremental underpinnings as refuse and waste are really telling. The dump, in effect, contains (though it is uncontainable, a pure excess and a perpetual self-overflow) everything that is rejected, or, following the argument of my *Energy Dreams*, it piles up the broken shells of the actual after the valuable kernel of potentiality they had held was extracted. This excess also encompasses everything that is excluded from the purview of use and, though useless or indifferent toward utilization, is genuinely valued in capital's semantico-economic regime. The tremendous quanta of energy wasted in flaring or in the generation of cryptocurrencies, such as the bitcoin, spell out the meaning of energy in the age of the dump, which is the material shadow of the immaterial, abstract, practically useless value. So, the main sources of pollution are not to be sought in purposeful use (of transportation, for instance) but in the purposeless (from the standpoint of use) burning up of the world.

In an unconscious inversion, the rejected is the only thing that is accepted without accepting it; in the dump, everything is refuse, the difference between the precious kernel and the discardable shell leveled. It is a consequence of extractivism, which invariably participates in excretive activities, forcing at its ground zero the earth to excrete the contents of its bowels in the shape of whatever is mined, from metals to fossils, and then to prolong the trail of this geo-excretion into the atmosphere thanks to the process of combustion or into the oceans through the byproducts of petrochemical industries. "It is possible," writes Freud, "that the contrast between the most precious substance known to men and the most worthless, which they reject as waste matter ('refuse'), has led to this specific identification of gold with feces" (SE 9: 174).

Nearly ten years subsequent to his essay on character and anal erotism, Freud will revisit the topic in another mini-paper, "On Transformations of

Instinct as Exemplified in Anal Erotism" (1917). The main question of this later work is crucial to psychoanalysis in general, namely: what is the fate of the expressions of instinctual impulses after, in the course of individual development, previous modes of expression are overcome? "Do they preserve their original nature, but in a state of repression? Are they sublimated or assimilated by transformation into character-traits?" (SE 17: 127–8). And so forth. In the case of anal erotism, these questions and the answers they point to are complicated by the fact that the retentive aspect of this stage militates against further development, so that the problem needs to be restated in terms of the need to change the ideally unchangeable, to metabolize the non-metabolizable. Expression and repression, attraction and disgust, as well as release and withholding, are now joined by decay and non-decomposition as the structuring contradictions of mental and material realities of the dump. For instance, when the techno-excrement of industrial production starts having ecosystem-wide and organism-shaping effects, then the dump comes to dictate the rules of the game of life. Made primarily of plastic, the Great Pacific Garbage Patch becomes home to entire communities of coastal creatures, and nuclear isotopes with half-lives reaching into thousands of years induce genetic mutations.

The main contribution of Freud's 1917 paper is, however, a reconceptualization of anal erotism in terms of the dynamics of detachment and attachment. Whether feces are symbolically viewed as a gift, a baby, or a penis—all of them "ill-distinguished from one another" from the standpoint of the unconscious (SE 17: 128)—the desire to withhold them and thus to keep them as an integral part of oneself or to release and externalize them into the world vacillates between the poles of attachment and detachment. In the interplay of these opposites, spatial and psychic relations become possible. A fetish is the case of extreme (physical) detachment, in which attachment is purely symbolic. Primary narcissism is the case of extreme attachment. These extremes are, for Freud, not deviations from but the foundations for the transformations of instinct traceable to anal erotism: "the infantile wish for a penis [. . .] changes into the wish for a *man*, and thus puts up with the man as an appendage to the penis" (SE 17: 129). The logic of the fetish as a detachable part (experienced either in the fear of its permanent physical detachment as in castration anxiety, or in the situational uses within the logic of replacements, or, again, in the moment of fecal release)—hence, the vegetal logic of the fetish, seeing that plants consist almost entirely of detachable and replaceable organs—underpins the subsequent attachments and assemblages that never break with this initial mechanism.

If, in the world, or the unworld, of the dump, relations are the preeminent victims, that is because the differences, spatiotemporal distances, and articulations of attachment and detachment are no longer operative there. The indifferent lumping together of rests that resist decomposition, suffusion of ecosystems and organisms with toxic substances, or exposure to radiation render everything and everyone equally attached to *and* detached from themselves, each other, and the overall dump. The dump does not amount to a whole and, therefore, has no parts, regardless of a careful study which may individuate its components. Whereas in each singular instance of relationality it is true that detachment *is* attachment, in formal terms, the absolute equation of the two poles destroys the conditions of possibility for relationality. The same holds for the direct coincidence of fecal retention and massive release in the dump.

Both here and in *Dump Philosophy*, Freud's notion of anal erotism is adapted to the erotism of the dump. One further conclusion may be drawn about the "gift theory" of feces, which I have not yet dealt with. The process of their externalization and detachment viewed as a gift to the outside world implicitly connects the organismic body and the body of the earth. Manure is, indeed, a gift to the soil, enriching it with nitrogen, granting it fertility, and converting that which is apparently useless and disgusting into a valuable nourishment "from below" for future life. But, in the age of the dump, nothing remains unaffected, and the fecal matter of both human beings and domestic animals is replete with traces of pharmaceutical products, antibiotics, heavy metals (copper, cadmium, zinc), chemical pesticides and herbicides, etc. (This is not to mention tons of objects that should not be flushed down the drains but that are nevertheless dumped into the sewage system.) Many of these cannot be removed in wastewater- and sewage-treatment facilities; aspects of the dump remain constant across the process of ingestion-excretion, as much as between the bodies of individual organisms and the skin of the earth that is the topsoil.

E

Environment, "external world," eco-psycho-analysis

In Freudian psychoanalysis, "the external world" (*Aussenwelt*) stands for everything that reaches the ego via the perceptual apparatus. It is a reality, which is independent of the psychological subject, but which imposes its own demands and enables the satisfaction or, more frequently, spells out the dissatisfaction of wishes and desires. There is no sense, from the psychoanalytic standpoint, to inquire into the being of this reality; in the section of *An Outline of Psychoanalysis* devoted to "the external world," Freud admits in a Kantian vein: "Reality will always remain 'unknowable'" (SE 23: 196). Yet, one cannot disregard its demands and the limitations it imposes, just as one cannot disregard those of the impulses arising from the unconscious. The ego, as a result, is in the "intermediate position between the external world and the id" (SE 19: 149), as Freud notes in a succinct 1923 essay, "Neurosis and Psychosis."

The position of the ego is essentially intermediate: it stands in the middle between two non-objectifiable domains, and from that middle with neither beginning nor end relates to the oft-conflicting demands of the inner and the outer worlds. More than that, its position is essentially superficial. Consciousness is extended, embodied, and embedded; it is "the *surface* of the mental apparatus" and "is spatially the first one reached from the external world" (SE 19: 19). The inner truth of its extendedness is the unconscious, of which it is an outgrowth. At the porous boundary between the inner and the outer, the psychoanalytic ego is an ecological subject, which emerges when a part of the unconscious is shaped by its milieu. Succinctly put, THE EGO IS ECO; it is, by virtue of what it is, non-egoistic. "The ego is that part of the id," Freud contends, "which has been modified by the direct influence of the external world through the medium of the *Pcpt.-Cs.*" (SE 19: 25). There is no psychological subject without the surfacing of the middle, without the interface of different surfaces, whose interrelations, tensions, and synergies bring "me" into existence. Despite the designation "depth psychology," the psychoanalytic method also begins from the middle and from the surface, or the interface, following the ecological (and vegetal) development of its subject: "Our investigation too must take this perceiving surface as our starting-point" (SE 19: 19).

Once constituted by the opposite pressures of the outer and the inner worlds, without any substantive reality of its own, the ego worries about reconciling mutually incompatible demands, integrating, mending the fabric of mental life. Its relation to external reality remains animal- or plant-like: reality testing, informing the evolving reality principle, is described by Freud in his 1925 "Mystic Writing-Pad" essay, in terms of periodic extension and retraction of the surface-oriented elements of the mental apparatus: "It is as though the unconscious stretches out feelers, through the medium of the system *Pcpt.-Cs.*, towards the external world and hastily withdraws them as soon as they have sampled the excitations coming from it. [...] The discontinuous method of functioning of the system *Pcpt.-Cs.* lies at the bottom of the origin of the concept of time" (SE 19: 231).[1]

The mediations of the ego reveal that it is a medium, or even an instrument in the service of the unconscious (albeit an instrument, which is not strictly separate from the unconscious, whose own specialized organ it is) for getting in touch with external reality as an insect does with its antennae or a plant with its sensitive and probing root tips. A vital relation, this is not an indissoluble bond, but an immanently interrupted engagement, a halting rhythm of approaches and retreats, without which there is no time. (Given that the unconscious "itself" does not come in touch with external reality, for it, from its perspective, time does not pass nor even exists.) Neuroses and psychoses are the vicissitudes of the uncertain and precarious nature of the ego qua relation, the relation that is inherently self-disrupted and self-disrupting.

Schematically, Freud suggests that *"neurosis is the result of a conflict between the ego and its id, whereas psychosis is the analogous outcome of a similar disturbance in the relations between the ego and the external world"* (SE 19: 149). The negation of the validity, veracity, or significance of the external world in metaphysical philosophy, arguing for this world's mere epiphenomenality, is, therefore, a symptom of psychosis. As in psychosis, a metaphysical philosopher "creates, autocratically, a new external and internal world" (SE 19: 151), the authentic world of ideas, God, spirit, substance, or the idealist subject. In turn, the extreme repression of carnal desires and passions situates metaphysical philosophy and theology in the camp of neurosis. Whatever the diagnosis, the anti- or non-ecological subject is doubly alienated from the environment and from its own affective life; this subject widens the gap at the core of all relations—and, above all, of the relational ego—until this gap is transformed into an abyss.

Something of a split into psychotic and neurotic approaches is detectable in the current environmental crisis. In psychosis, points of access to the external world are blocked and "the id's wishful impulses" orchestrate the creation of an alternative reality, leading to dissociation in situations of frustration and non-fulfillment (SE 19: 151). Unconscious wishful constructions ignore all scientific and other types of evidence. Convictions that there is no climate change and it is all one big conspiracy of "deep state"; that "natural resources" are infinite and may be mined with impunity in previously untouched zones of the planet or in outer space; that burning fossils, or other materials, en masse poses no ecological threats weave together a parallel reality, expressive of unbridled unconscious desires. Insofar as they gain a certain degree of inner consistency, such convictions manage to put the ego in their service, replacing a relation to the external world with delusions: "a fair number of analyses have taught us that the delusion is found applied like a patch over the place where originally a rent had appeared in the ego's relation to the external world" (SE 19: 151). This generic technique applies not only to climate change denial but also to the psychotic denial of ethnic, sexual, or other kinds of difference within contemporary societies. For its part, neoliberal ideology indeed disavows the climate crisis in an incomplete detachment from the external world (SE 19: 153).[2]

At the other end of the spectrum, neuroses repudiate the demands of the id and, as we will see, feign total disregard for the pleasure principle (SE 19: 152). Taking the challenges and existential menace of catastrophic climate change seriously may impel one to renege on pleasure and to insist on the most austere and self-sacrificial conduct. Pleasure is then sadistically or sadomasochistically sought from self-abnegation. The case for the cessation of air travel, rather than efforts to limit the number of flights per year or to reimagine the technologies of flying that would be less damaging to the atmosphere, is a symptom of climate neurosis. The same holds for climate taxation models that would make the most economically vulnerable pay a lion's share of the costs involved in the energy transition and related measures. Paradoxically, a climate neurosis may push a significant portion of the population in the direction of a climate psychosis, assuming that the stark choice is between allegiance with the superego and the external world or with the id. Instead of fostering polarization, it would be advisable to renegotiate afresh our relation to the external world, on the one hand, and to desires, on the other, in the age of a severe environmental crisis and climate change. In the course of such a renegotiation, the ego would be reinvented, recalibrating the middle where it is and *that* it is, instead of surrendering to one of the opposing poles it is slotted between.

We may glimpse alternative attitudes to the external world in *Civilization and Its Discontents*, namely in its discussion of the "oceanic feeling," which is a term Romain Rolland coined in his 1927 letter to Freud. "It is a feeling," Freud relates, "which he would like to call a sensation of 'eternity,' a feeling as of something limitless, unbounded—as it were, 'oceanic'" (SE 21: 64). Freud confesses that he "cannot discover this 'oceanic' feeling" in himself and further specifies it as "a feeling of an indissoluble bond, of being one with the external world as a whole" (SE 21: 65). The questioning of the Cartesian split between the body and the mind, as well as between the subject and the world, seems to affirm the bond, as does also a holistic understanding of ecology. Yet, like psychosis and neurosis, this feeling also requires that one give up on the middle, letting go of the ego not as a rigid mental structure but as the mediator and an interface between the internal and the external worlds.

Fusion, furthermore, is not yet (or already not) a relation—Freud is right to detect in it traces of narcissism. It is, according to him, either a pathology or a sign of being in love, when "against all the evidence of his senses, a man who is in love declares that 'I' and 'you' are one" (SE 21: 66). Does oceanic feeling imply the ecological affect of "love of the world"?[3] If the answer is *yes*, then one should be prepared to love the world not as a pristine ideal, but just as it is: full of microplastics, murderous and genocidal impulses and actions, floods and wars, global heating and abject poverty. In a sense, the love of the "real" world with all its grotesque, dispiriting, even disgusting features is at the heart of the Christian message and of divine *kenosis* in mortal flesh. But the typical ecological rendition of the oceanic feeling is idealizing, resulting in a fusion with an egoic projection overshadowed by secondary narcissism.

To return to Freud's distinction between neuroses and psychoses, in a 1924 follow-up paper, "The Loss of Reality in Neurosis and Psychosis," a puzzling similarity between the two seemingly polarized conditions is pinpointed: like psychosis, "every neurosis disturbs the patient's relation to reality in some way" (SE 19: 183). A curious implication of neurosis is that *in the name of the reality principle* one loses one's relation to reality. Freud cites compensatory mechanisms for the severe (and failed at that) repression of the ego as the reason behind this loss; however, the structural factor is the ego's abandonment of its essentially intermediate position on the surface, or at the interface, between external and internal worlds. There is no access to reality without the intermediacy of the ego, that is to say, without a connection to the unconscious realm of desires, phantasies, dreams. A forcefully neurotic response to the environmental crisis is, in its consequences, barely distinguishable from a psychotic reaction.

In keeping with the compensatory logic of environmental neuroses, individual and collective sacrifices and austerity measures, often decoupled from their actual effectiveness, are imbued with great significance. Virtue signaling is symptomatic here, in that it represents an effort to substitute the pleasures one has renounced, presumably for the good of the planet and for the sake of future generations, with pleasure derived from that very act of renunciation. This is what Freud calls "the attempt at reparation" (SE 19: 185), reintroducing the ego in the middle, between the reality principle it obeyed and the unconscious world it renounced (in the case of a neurosis), or between the reality it ignored and the unconscious call it heeded (in the case of a psychosis). In the last instance, though, "in neurosis, the initial obedience is succeeded by a deferred attempt at flight" (SE 19: 185), which, in the context of ecological action, is a flight into the non-reflexive urgency of having to do something *now* and the imputation of absolute, unquestionable meaning to the immediately undertaken or endorsed action (for instance, not questioning the environmental impact and the philosophical sense of nuclear energy as a good replacement for fossil fuels, resorting to strikes, or endorsing the language and mechanisms of debt repayment).

It is, nonetheless, a distinguishing feature of neurosis that "a piece of reality is avoided by a sort of flight, whereas in psychosis it is remodeled" (SE 19: 185). Unlike neurosis with its negative flight from reality, psychosis substitutes the rejected external world with one that is internally generated, while relying on a mesh of delusions and hallucinations, meant to supply cognitive and perceptual evidence for this generation (SE 19: 186). It is a singular challenge of eco-activism to steer clear of either neurotic or psychotic responses to the environmental crisis—that is, to avoid both the avoidance and the delusional substitution of external reality, reinforced by the echo chamber of closed communities, whether on- or offline.

To be sure, the lag between drastic changes in external reality and the mix of conscious and unconscious constructions of that reality is inevitable.

On the side of reality testing, the tentacular or antennal approaches to and retractions from the sampled excitations emanating from the world are not only intermittent, but also become less frequent, the more time is necessary for their processing and interpretation. When one ventures again to sample bits of the outside world, these may be unlike anything experienced before. In view of its own dynamics, reality testing cannot catch up with the rapid modifications of that which is tested: the lag increases, dictating the pace of time itself in the anachrony between the intermittencies of the system *Pcpt.-Cs.* and relentless environmental change.

On the side of the unconscious, the quasi-mythic constructions of external reality (pure and purifying water; infinitely regenerating nature, arising phoenix-like from fire and ashes, etc.) are monumentally fixed, oblivious to all evidence to the contrary. Here, change is not recognized as such. Because, for the unconscious, it as though no time passes at all, "nature" is stuck in an ahistorical present, where there is no contamination, mass extinction, the undermining of fragile supports for vitality, nor even mutations and evolution. The lag between atemporal unconscious space and rapidly accelerating change is absolute.

Effective eco-activism and the ego position it occupies have no other choice but to contend with the double challenge of conscious processes and unconscious incapacities to catch up with the external world. Informative as they may be, references to science, expert prognostications, and fact-checking will be of little help. At any rate, they ought to be supplemented with the analysis of resistances and, not least, with interminable self-analysis. The hermeneutical interpretation of facts is an unavoidable component of the endeavor: far from a "merely" subjective spin on hard environmental data, it is always implicated in the work of understanding, at times overtly and at other times covertly. And it is to be paired with interpretation in the psychoanalytic sense, linking manifest statements, images, thoughts, and emotions to their latent significance (SE 23: 165), which may outright contradict them, to the subsoil of the inner world implicated in whatever is asserted about the external world.

In texts on metapsychology, such as the 1915 "Instincts and Their Vicissitudes," the middling position of the ego is further divided down the middle, when Freud distinguishes the "reality-ego" from the "pleasure-ego" (SE 14: 136). Secondary narcissism depends on this distinction, which permits the subject to establish a self-relation, as does the ego's presumed self-sufficiency and auto-erotism. "In so far as the ego is auto-erotic, it has no need of the external world, but, in consequence of experiences undergone by the instincts of self-preservation, it acquires objects from that world, and, in spite of everything, it cannot avoid feeling internal instinctual stimuli for a time as unpleasurable" (SE 14: 135).

Is this not a portrait of the autonomous subject oblivious to the environment, one who holds the conviction of not needing the external world? If, however, experiences related to self-preservation expel the subject outside itself and practically demonstrate its dependence on "objects" in that world, then the shattering of the ego's auto-erotic idyll will be still more traumatic when the world, rather than isolated objects in it, is on the verge of disappearance. In psychological terms, the event of the anticipated loss of the external world deals a serious wound to narcissism and threatens the middle where the ego is (the middle *that* it is) with the possibility of imploding, of collapsing into itself.

The problem of the external world is thus not entirely external to the ego, formed at an interface between the world and the unconscious. It may be tempting to interpret the inclusion of the external world in terms of an expanded notion of narcissism, perhaps with an escape route leading all the way back to primary, infantile narcissism. The ego reestablishes its self-relation and auto-erotism by interpreting its relation to the external world as an integral part of a planetary, or even cosmic, narcissistic structure. The oceanic feeling follows the logic of an expanded narcissism, with the polymorphously perverse cosmic sexuality as its juicy flesh, which is threatened not *from* the outside but *on* the outside, taken to be, to a significant extent, inside, as the planetary womb of existence. Where instrumental considerations prevail over play, secondary narcissism is put into practice, as it is, for instance, in the argument that care for the planet and for other species is ultimately care for ourselves, in the present or the future ("future generations," for the sake of whom environmental ethical actions are to be carried out, are almost in all instances the future generations of *Homo sapiens*).

A more nuanced stance, faithful to the uncentered middle that is the ego is to treat the external world neither as an infinite extension of myself nor an entirely alien reality. In a 1917 paper, "A Difficulty in Psychoanalysis," Freud discusses the three blows to human narcissism: the cosmological blow dealt by the Copernican revolution, the biological blow emanating from the Darwinian theory of evolution, and the psychological blow (deriving from psychoanalysis), which puts the conscious subject in its very modest place (SE 18: 139–41). The fourth, ecological blow should be now added to the list. Freud's suggestion is not to rescue narcissistic illusions. Instead, he claims that psychoanalysis seeks "to educate the ego" (SE 18: 143) by putting it back in its place, in the middle, the *not-all*, from which it is so tempting to escape into the *all* of reality or of phantasy. His lesson for the ego "amount[s] to a statement that *the ego is not master in its own house*" (SE 18: 143), which is the deeper sense of ecology: the ego is still "*in its own house*" but in a position of non-mastery and non-proprietorship: its own house is not its own. Dwelling in the middle, the ego is in touch with exteriority that is also within, albeit never fully interiorized or introjected.

F

Fetishism and the climate

In the 1905 *Three Essays on the Theory of Sexuality*, Freud includes a concise statement on the subject of fetishism. "There are some cases," he writes there, "which are quite specially remarkable—those in which the normal sexual object is replaced by another which bears some relation to it, but is entirely unsuited to serve the normal sexual aim" (SE 7: 153). Freud will soon qualify his assertion by commenting that a certain degree of fetishism is "habitually present in normal love" and that pathologies emerge when a fetish "*takes the place* of the normal aim, and, further, when the fetish becomes detached from a particular individual and becomes the *sole* object" (SE 7: 154). The emphasis on normalcy is to be comprehended within the teleological trajectory ending in genital sexuality, which Freud charts. A fetish could, however, be a remnant of infantile polymorphous perversity, in which the entire body is sexualized. What distinguishes it from a sexually significant body part in polymorphous perversity is the very feature that makes the fetish problematic, namely its capacity to be symbolically detached from and to replace the love object.

Aspects of the planetary environmental crisis are fetishized in the precise sense of becoming detached from and replacing the whole. Prominently, the climate and climate change function as fetishes of the environmental crisis. In turn, the fetishization of climate change is its replacement with average planetary temperature rises (e.g., the 1.5C discussed at COP 21 in Paris), detached from the whole they are a part of. Here and elsewhere, scientific and statistical operationalization of complex realities smuggles in fetishism, masquerading as a true representation of the world as it is. And let us not forget that the exclusive focus on ecology is, likewise, fetishistic: it obfuscates the crisis of metaphysical thought and its metastases of instrumental rationality, capital, or extractive-destructive energy, among others.

The climate is not so much a hyperobject, as Timothy Morton has claimed;[1] it is more of a *hyperfetish*. The aporia of the climate fetish is that, as an all-encompassing, all-involving condition, the climate is by definition not a detachable part, which may replace the whole bearing "some relation to it." Nevertheless, across a range of responses to the climate crisis, it is treated as though it were a manipulable object (that is, a fetish) to be adjusted, tuned, engineered at will. The apparatus and the logic responsible for the objectification of and control over a piece of external reality are concentrated on the climate issue, which is precisely unobjectifiable. The climate is also a fetish of the planetary crisis because the vicious cycle of technogenic industrial or energy byproducts and technological solutions gyrates around it. The possibility of regaining control over the uncontrollable consequences of the apparently complete human control over the environment stands or falls on climate change (and a planned, directed, steered change of that change).

Freud analyzes fetishism insofar as it operates in sexual objects and in situations of sexual attraction. He does, at the same time, compare the procedures of substitutions, by means of which fetishism works, "to the fetishes in which savages believe that their gods are embodied" (SE 7: 153). Putting aside the historically conditioned language for referring to animist traditions, it becomes clear that the fetish is endowed with tremendous significance. Already, for a part to attain a certain measure of independence (symbolic or otherwise) from the whole that it will replace and not to dissipate in continuous fragmentation, it must concentrate a great deal of power, guaranteeing its position. This power, we might add, is that of an indirect representation: of the crisis of metaphysical thought and its repercussions by the environmental crisis; of the environment by the climate; of climate change by numeric measures of temperature increases ... The embodiment of power in a fetish depends on the amassing and constant backsliding of cathexes, so much so that the fetishized part becomes more cathected than the whole, from which it is detached and which it replaces. This is what happens with the fetish of the climate and especially of the quantifications of its change: heated discussions about tipping points and points of no return, about curbing temperature rises to 1.5C, about climate debt and climate finance are hyper-cathected *at the expense of (and as a compensation for) that which they replace.*

Why does a fetishist transfer focus, power, efficacy, and cathexes from the sexual object to a fetish? Why, in other words, is the fetish more appealing than the object it substitutes for? Freud's answer in a 1927 short essay is that "the fetish is a substitute for a penis," particularly "for the woman's (the mother's) penis that the little boy once believed in and—for reasons familiar to us—does not want to give up" (SE 21: 152–3). Ultimately, a fetish replaces an absent object, a non-existent one, or, in our case, a non-object, such as the climate. It is a way to both hold onto and to let go of a frustrated phantasy by means of what Freud will term *Verleugnung,* "disavowal." So, the fetish of temperature increases disavows climate change, the fetish of the climate disavows the environment, and, most importantly, the fetish of the environmental crisis disavows metaphysics. In this last (or first, depending on the perspective) instance, the power of the fetish is properly phantasmatic: it is "designed to preserve [. . .] from extinction" (SE 21: 152) a phantasy, which nevertheless produces a plethora of effects in the "real world." The de-contextualized, isolated view of the environmental crisis is a disavowed remainder of metaphysics, as are the objectifying approaches to the climate and technological solutions to technogenic problems.

It is very likely that pointing out the connection between metaphysics and its fetishist disavowal in the environmental crisis would trigger consternation and skepticism that are similar to those aroused by Freud's claim about the disavowal of the maternal penis. Aside from the usual resistances, incredulity and aversion are built into the structure of disavowal: "an aversion, which is never absent in any fetishist, to the real female genitals remains a *stigma indelebile* of the repression that has taken place" (SE 21: 154). Each symbolic link between the fetish and what it fetishizes is buried in the unconscious, its cathexes transferred over to the fetish, which is, consequently, invested with its incomparable power. In relations of representation (say, of climate change by average global temperature increases) the link is transparent, but a thick and obscure underside of the unrepresentable and the unrepresented makes such relations possible—and it is here that repression and resistances to lifting it are most active.

The power of the fetish also goes two ways. On the one hand, it is the fetish's power over fetishists, unable to deal with their desire save for the mediations of the fetish. On the other hand, it is the power of the fetishist, who "can readily obtain the sexual satisfaction attached to it [to the fetish, MM]. What other men have to woo and make exertions for can be had by the fetishist with no trouble at all" (SE 21: 154). Each instance of fetishist disavowal arrogates power to the fetish: to numeric measures and models, to the climate, to the environmental crisis, commanding much of the conscious attention of the fetishists that we are. But each of these instances also empowers fetishists, making it easier to manage such unwieldy notions as the environment, the climate, and its catastrophic change. The empowerment is rather deceptive, however: for sexual fetishists, a fetish "is seldom felt [. . .] as the symptom of an ailment accompanied by suffering" (SE 21: 152), and for eco-fetishists, the successive reduction, operationalization, and displacement of what the fetish disavows is seldom sensed as a problem. It would be fair to say, then, that the dual power of the fetish also empowers *and* disempowers, or, more exactly, disempowers in empowering action and comprehension alike.

In this regard, Freud speaks of an interruption of the gaze, frozen and monumentalized by the fetish, which is a prominent case of fixation. "It seems," he notes, "that when the fetish is instituted some process occurs which reminds one of the stopping of memory in traumatic amnesia. As in this latter case, the subject's interest comes to a halt half-way, as it were; it is as though the last impression before the uncanny and traumatic one is retained as a fetish" (SE 21: 155). The gliding of the glance, which Freud describes, from the shoe and foot, up the leg to the underwear and pubic hair (fur and velvet), creates a whole scale of fetishes, upon which the glance is fixed and libidinal energy is fixated at a greater or lesser remove from the disavowed maternal penis. Similarly, the ecological glance slides along and halts at the numeric measures of temperature rises, climate change, climate, and the environmental crisis, often blamed on Western colonialism, capitalism, anthropocentrism, constructions of masculinity, or heteronormativity. The "uncanny and traumatic" stage of the metaphysical mode of thinking and being (not as phallic tyranny, but, precisely, as the absent, always-already castrated phallus) is never reached, the theoretical glance stopping at the "last impression" before that stage.

Freud remarks that the most effective fetishes, and the most durable at that, are those "doubly derived from contrary ideas," such as an "athletic support-belt which could also be worn as bathing drawers. This piece of clothing covered up the genitals entirely and concealed the distinction between them" (SE 21: 156–7). The next step, never taken in fetishism, of beholding what is behind the screen of the support belt leads to the indeterminate notion that "women were castrated and that they were not castrated; and it also allowed of the hypothesis that men were castrated" (SE 21: 156). The indeterminacy of the root force behind the fetish is not only an either/or choice, but also a both/and, even when mutually exclusive options are involved. Hence, with the eco-fetish, the world is castrated and not castrated by metaphysics: the fragile conditions of possibility for life are undermined and the quality of life is overall improving thanks to techno-scientific advances. And metaphysics itself is castrated and not castrated; it is an effortlessly identifiable body of thought, of canonical texts, which may be simply "canceled" for being politically incorrect according to contemporary standards, and an omnipotent web of institutions, "commonsense" beliefs into which metaphysical ideas have morphed, presuppositions and desires in effect today. The oft-cited sentence from Friedrich Hölderlin—"But where the danger lies, there also grows a saving power"—belongs together with fetishist disavowal.

When Freud returns to the theme of fetishism in his posthumously published *Outline of Psychoanalysis*, he characterizes it as a "compromise" formation, assigned "the role of the penis which he [the fetishist, MM] cannot do without" (SE 23: 203). Could it be that we cannot do without metaphysics—that is, without reducing everything to one all-determining, all-encompassing reality? If so, then the various fetishes, even when highly critical of metaphysical totalization, are actually compromise formations furnishing no more than its symbolic substitutes. To give up on the temptation to totalize and to reduce complexity to a simple Cause, absolute origin, or certain end is, according to the internalized metaphysical scheme, tantamount to castration. Yet, in their indisputable multiplicity, all substitutes smuggle with them exactly this bit of metaphysical logic, relegated to numbers, the-one-thing-that-rules-all, a single eschatology, and so on. "The creation of the fetish was due to an intention to destroy the evidence for the possibility of castration" (SE 23: 203), but this possibility is maintained alive and destroyed by the very fetish that was meant to be a sign of reassurance.

G

Geo-psycho-analysis

"Geopsychoanalysis and 'the rest of the world'" is the title of a lecture, which Jacques Derrida delivered at the opening of a Franco-Latin American meeting in Paris in February 1981. At the start of the lecture, Derrida announces that he will not "propose a psychoanalysis of the earth," as Gaston Bachelard did in two volumes dedicated to this element.[1] Nor, with the exception of two brief references to Freud, does he engage with psychoanalytic thought, but, rather, with psychoanalytic organizations, societies, and associations that divide the earth into geographical regions, repeating certain geopolitical and even colonial gestures. I hyphenate geo-psycho-analysis to mark the distance between this apparently twin term to Derrida's.

So, what is geo-psycho-analysis? Different schools of psychoanalysis acknowledge that the infants' earliest ties to the outside world are based on their interactions with the primary caregiver, traditionally a mother. When the earth is called "mother earth," *Pachamama, Bhudevi, Atabei,* or *Gaia,* this should be taken to the letter—not as a mythical personification, but as everything that the relation to the mother entails in psychic life. Geo-psycho-analysis is Gaia-psycho-analysis.

Freud gives a rare indication of the psychological significance of "mother earth" in a passage from *Inhibitions, Symptoms, Anxiety,* which I have already cited. His words are worth recalling in the present context: "As soon as writing, which entails making a liquid flow of a tube on to a piece of white paper, assumes the significance of copulation, or as soon as walking becomes a symbolic substitute for treading upon the body of mother earth, both writing and walking are stopped because they represent the performance of a forbidden sexual act" (SE 20: 90).

When walking "becomes a symbolic substitute for treading on the body of mother earth," this treading itself is a stand-in for "the performance of a forbidden sexual act." At the very least, the Oedipal framework orients the interpretation of the *desire* for mother earth, which is consummated when the father is killed. Now, if the paternal figure is the sky, Ouranos, or the God of monotheism, then the death of God, which Nietzsche announces in the nineteenth century, is only a prelude to the event of consummating the relation to mother earth with unlimited industrial development, drilling, mining, fracking, not only treading upon but boring into her body, phallically entering and, in fact, creating holes in it, so as to reunite with it—or to a voyeuristic observation of these activities from a philosophical point of view.[2] Even the demand to abstain from extractivism, to "keep it in the ground," negatively alludes to the phallic potential of combustibles and of the technologies that bring this potential to the surface, taking it out of the planetary pants, as it were. The love professed for mother earth ought to be examined under the psychoanalytic lens as an incestuous relation to the mother, in which differences between the ecologically minded and the defenders of heedless exploitation of natural resources are not as sharply delineated as they tend to be. More than that, it is necessary to ask: who is *that*, mother earth after the death of the father?

Another rare reference to mother earth crops up in *Totem and Taboo* (1913). Here, it is not industrialization but the invention of agriculture that serves as a model for the sons taking the place of the murdered father god: "The son's efforts to put himself in the place of the father god became even more obvious. The introduction of agriculture increased the son's importance in the patriarchal family. He ventured upon new demonstrations of his incestuous libido, which found symbolic satisfaction in his cultivation of Mother Earth" (SE 13: 152). Agriculture is the replacement of the sex act with mother earth, whose fertility is stimulated by ploughs and pitchforks, instead of her amorous union with the celestial father god. Freud cites "divine figures such as Attis, Adonis and Tammuz," those "spirits of vegetation and at the same time youthful divinities enjoying the favors of the mother goddess and committing incest with their mother in defiance of the father" (SE 13: 152), but even the biblical Noah is cast in a similar light in mystical Jewish interpretations, including in the medieval book of *Zohar*. The theological-patriachal outlines of the Oedipal triangle emerge in incestuous proximity to mother earth, subsequent to the murder of the divine father.

From the invention of agriculture to the Industrial Revolution, geo-psycho-analysis suggests, every large-scale technological advance has come about in the footsteps of the death of a god, the murder of the divine father, and the interposition of the human agricultural or industrial communities (represented by "youthful divinities") in his place with respect to mother earth. Most recently, we might add, it is capital itself, which dissolves every communal bond, that has replaced the murdered father god. Further, the matrix of the Oedipus complex is suffused with guilt. "The sense of guilt," Freud writes, "found expression in myths which granted only short lives to these youthful favorites of the mother-goddesses and decreed their punishment by emasculation or by the wrath of the father in the form of an animal" (SE 13: 152). The sense of eco-guilt may be found in the same constellation, in which large-scale technologies penetrating into and polluting the earth, the oceans, and the atmosphere are the prostheses of the main actors of the Anthropocene. In addition to the ecological havoc it wreaks, the global environmental crisis is collective emasculation, experienced (at the unconscious level) as a punishment for the event precipitating the death of God and for the incestuous intercourse with mother earth.

Although in his anthropological observations Freud often relies on accounts of missionaries and colonizers, he is able to gauge the cross-cultural severity of the prohibition *and* the temptation of incest. In heterosexual cases, "psychoanalysis has taught us," he notes, "that a boy's earliest choice of objects for his love is incestuous and that those objects are forbidden ones—his mother and his sister. We have learnt, too, the manner in which, as he grows up, he liberates himself from this incestuous attraction" (SE 13: 17). The liberation in question is never complete: the strategy is to replace the earliest chosen objects with other ones, to deflect desire to a "safer" object who resembles, in one way or another, the original. It follows that, *mutatis mutandis*, it is forbidden to love the earth insofar as she is a mother; the love of mother earth would be incestuous *in patriarchal societies, where humanity plays the role of her son, rather than of her daughter.* This same love would be channeled otherwise in matriarchal societies, even if, consistent with geo-psycho-analysis it would be subject to other vicissitudes, such as those of the Electra complex. Be this as it may, farming and industrial production are the half-hearted deflections of the original object choice.

Already in the 1905 work, *Three Essays on the Theory of Sexuality*, Freud comments on incestual desire in a section dedicated to a study of "the barrier against incest." While Freud believes that the prohibition of incest is so ancient as to have "become established in many persons by organic inheritance" (SE 7: 225, fn3), he also points out that the period of puberty is there to "loosen their [notably the adolescent boys', MM] connection with their family" and to exclude in practice their parents from their scope of their object-choice (SE 7: 225). How does this pertain to the object-choice of another, greater mother, namely mother earth?

So long as we continue to live in the earthly, terrestrial fold, separation from her is impossible. At the same time, voyages into outer space and to other planets (dreamt of in various texts of Russian cosmism, for instance, and realized in the middle of the twentieth century) signal a detachment from mother earth, if not at the physical level for the vast majority of its human inhabitants, then at least at the level of the perspective and the gaze, now trained to see our planet from a distance, say, from the moon, as in the photographs of "The Blue Marble" or "Earthrise."[3] Based on the logic of Russian cosmism or its ideological perversions in Elon Musk's immodest proposal on the subject of "making humanity a multiplanetary species,"[4] separation from the planet, albeit symbolic and mediated by the techno-gaze of satellites, ushers in the puberty of humankind. Connection with mother earth is loosened in what Freud construes as "one of the most significant, but also one of the most painful, psychical achievements of the pubertal period," which is "detachment from parental authority" (SE 7: 227).

For the proponents of cosmism and of human multiplanetarity, a stubborn attachment to mother earth is symptomatic of an infantile libidinal fixation, an incestuous desire to be united, or reunited, with the mother despite a series of successive separations beginning at birth. To be sure, this desire does persist in the realm of "phantasies, that is, in ideas that are not destined to be carried into effect" (SE 7: 226). And it is in phantasy that, against all odds, the multiplanetarists and the monoplantarists (the slogan "There Is No Planet B!" corresponds to the acknowledgment that there is only one mother, although her substitutes and stand-ins populate much of psychic life) meet on common ground.

Whether endorsing the physical and affective separation from or immersion in planet earth, the dream is to take the place of the father in an incestuous relation with the mother: in the case of multiplanetarists, to replace the sky itself, Ouranos, as the partner of Gaia; in the case of monoplanetarists, to return to the womb of mother earth, though not as embryos gestating there, but as individuals and species. Multiplanetarists do take a step further when they base their planetary object choice on the paradigmatic connection to mother earth. Freud observes that "there can be no doubt that every object-choice whatever is based, though less closely, on these prototypes" of the mother and the father (SE 7: 228), so that, instead of mother earth, multiplanetarists seek *other earths*, which would serve as substitutes for the planetary mother. Their step beyond resembles the transformation of an incestuous libidinal fixation into adult object choice (SE 7: 228).

In the structure of the Oedipus complex, the act of substitution affects both the mother and the father figures: "The hatred of his father that arises in a boy from rivalry for his mother is not able to achieve uninhibited sway over his mind [. . .] The child finds relief from the conflict arising out of this double-sided, this ambivalent emotional attitude towards his father by displacing his hostile and fearful feelings onto a *substitute* for his father" (SE 13: 129). Omnipotent patriarchal divinity is the closest father substitute, onto which hostile, fearful, and admiration-suffused feelings are displaced. When the figure of the human or the posthuman, the *anthropos* of the Anthropocene with technological might and sweeping influence over the entire planet, is put in its place, then the same mix of hostility and admiration is projected onto this figure, claiming to be its own father. Other candidates for the displacement of ambivalence toward the father are global capital and Western metaphysics, eclipsing and taking the place of the sun, which "is nothing but another sublimated symbol of the father" (SE 12: 54).

The last line is from Freud's analysis of the Schreber case. Diagnosed as a paranoiac psychotic, Judge Schreber breaks out the Oedipal triangle (and is fêted for that in Deleuze and Guattari's *Anti-Oedipus*), which means that he does not harbor incestuous desires toward the mother. Rather, faced with the parental couple of the solar masculine deity and mother earth (the sun's "counterpart in this picture of the two parents is 'Mother Earth' as she is generally called" [SE 7: 54]), Schreber *identifies with* the mother: "Dr. Schreber may have formed a phantasy that if he were a woman, he would manage the business of having children more successfully; and he may have thus found his way back to the feminine attitude towards his father" (SE 12: 58). That is, Schreber merges with mother earth not in an incestuous relation but in an attempt to become her. This would be a non- or anti-Oedipal interpretation of calls to return to Gaia—fusing with her, becoming her—but, in the process, accepting her position vis-à-vis the sun, celestial divinity, or capital, and, moreover, accepting this position *as one's own*.

Another variation on the non-Oedipal reconnection with mother earth is mediated by the death drive, instead of the sexual instinct, by Thanatos, rather than Eros. Musing over the theme of the three caskets in Shakespeare's *The Merchant of Venice*, Freud posits that mother earth, as the third instantiation of the mother, is none other than the goddess of death. "We might argue," Freud writes in the culmination of his analysis, "that what is represented here are the three inevitable relations that a man has with a woman—the woman who bears him, the woman who is his mate and the woman who destroys him; or that they are the three forms taken by the figure of the mother in the course of a man's life—the mother herself, the beloved one who is chosen after her pattern, and lastly the Mother Earth who receives him once more" (SE 12: 301).

Contrary to Freud's assertion, the second form is not "inevitable" there where heteronormativity does not rule the day. Could the non-inevitability of the second mother (a mate resembling one's female biological progenitor) have been retrospectively reflected onto the first and prospectively onto the third mothers? Assuming this scenario, the "true" birth would not hinge on the mother, as it also does *not* in philosophy from Plato to Hannah Arendt, from the myth of the cave to natality, which calls for the event of the other birth, the political and fully human emergence together with others in speech and deed. Likewise, the death, or the delivery of the body back to mother earth, would not be inevitable and aspirations to immortality would derive from the same source as dreams of a birth without the mother.

If, conversely, mother earth is the womb and the tomb of finite-terrestrial existence, then the ecological appeal to return to Gaia should be given its due also as the ground, from which everything arises and to which everything returns, the soil, into which remnants of past organic existence are composted welcoming the growth to come. Listing the three iterations of the mother, Freud does not discriminate between her erotic and thanatological connotations; indeed, the two drives (life and death) converge at a vanishing point on the horizon of mother earth. Perhaps unbeknownst to himself, he thereby breaks out of the Oedipal prisonhouse, replete with the connotations of patriarchy and rigid distinctions between opposite domains. Granted, in Freud's recounting of the story of King Lear, "eternal wisdom, clothed in the primeval myth, bids the old man renounce love, choose death and make friends with the necessity of dying" (SE 12: 301), and yet this same wisdom conveys more than this flat, lopsided choice (the theme of choosing is insistently replayed in this short text) in Freud's own reading of Shakespeare: at the end of the day, the embrace of death is of a piece with the strivings of love, both of them embodied in the figure of the mother.

A de-idealized image of mother earth, with soil and organic decomposition in the foreground, reemerges in the preface, which Freud wrote for the German translation of John Gregory Bourke's 1891 book, *Scatological Rites of All Nations*. There, Freud resorts to a quote from Goethe's *Faust* on the "trace of the earth" (*Erdenrest*), persisting in us, "of which the sexual and excretory functions remain a nucleus" (SE 12: 336). Of course, these functions are immediately recognizable as the nucleus of Freudian psychoanalysis and of the Aristotelian vegetal psychic faculty, *to threptikon*. Embarrassment with and concealment of this earthy trace is a symptom of repression, cutting us off from the earth itself (or, rather, herself) and, given the denial of our innermost relation to her, depriving us of ways of love *and* death.

"It must be said," Freud continues, "that the chief finding from psychoanalytic research has been the fact that the human infant is obliged to recapitulate during the early part of his development the changes in the attitude of the human race toward excremental matters which probably had their start when

Homo sapiens first raised himself off Mother Earth" (SE 12: 336). In human evolution and in one of the milestones of infancy, bipedal posture hierarchically situates the earth underneath—not underneath a horizontally positioned trunk of the body, but underfoot. The soil and everything soiled, dirt and excrements, "sexual and excretory functions," and/as mother earth are then no longer something one wallows in, but the lowest thing, physically and psychologically, abhorred, rejected, *and* unconsciously desired. But even if we are already not or not yet in it, the trace of the earth lingers on in us, so much so that it makes up the core of our psychic life.

The more the trace of the earth is repressed, the more it proliferates. With the unearthing and burning of fossils (oil, coal, natural gas), the earth is sent into the air as carbon monoxide and carbon dioxide, nitrogen, or sulfur dioxide. The trace of the earth is, in fact, everywhere: in the atmosphere and in the lungs, in the oceans filled with polyethylene and polypropylene and in drinking water. The embrace of mother earth is more encompassing—and more suffocating—the more we objectify it, putting ourselves over and against it. In light of the topological and archeological model of consciousness and the unconscious, it is as though the deep strata of the geological unconscious are immediately brought to bear on the present and the future: the fossils of long-dead animals and plants are still living at the behest of the extractive energy apparatus; they are chunks of the geological id that knows no passage of time. The incineration of the geological unconscious leads to climate deregulation, while the thin surface layer of the planet, which is propitious to life (the portion of geological consciousness), is encrusted with the non-decomposable remnants of that conflagration. In the Anthropocene, the earth displays traces of the earth as the traces of the human, who contains traces of the earth . . .

H

Hysteric conversions between organismic and ecological bodies

The studies of hysteria are among the earliest Freud undertook with Josef Breuer. Although his preferred method of treatment was still hypnosis, rather than the psychoanalytic "talking cure," and the conceptual apparatus of psychoanalysis was yet to be developed, the role of trauma and what will be later on understood as the unconscious mechanisms at its disposal were front and center in these studies.

The symptoms of hysteria are psychosomatic, grafted onto the body and its various parts (experienced in bodily tics, paralyses, neuralgias, and the like). This phenomenon is also called "hysterical conversion disorder." Psychical trauma does not just trigger the onset of symptoms; it persists and "acts like a foreign body which long after its entry must continue to be regarded as an agent that is still at work" (SE 2: 6). "We may reverse the dictum '*cessante causa cessat effectus*' ['when the cause ceases, the effect ceases'] and conclude from these observations that the determining process continues to operate in some way or other for years," Freud and Breuer add (SE 2: 7). The reversal of this dictum will become an axiom of psychoanalysis in general, with unconscious factors playing the role of "the determining process" of thinking, feeling, and behavior well after the trigger event.

Assuming that an ecosystem is also an extended mind, or a conjunction of modes of thinking corresponding to its various inhabitants and their interactions, ecological trauma does not merely (quasi-mechanically) disrupt ecosystems and push them to the point of collapse; rather, it provokes and continues operating environmental hysterical conversion disorders. The non-metabolizable materials released into the atmosphere, the earth, or bodies of water are the "determining processes" here, processes that sometimes take hundreds of years and that "act like a foreign body" within the milieu. More than either their physical perdurance or their synthetic-anthropogenic origins, it is the *failure to express them*, to articulate and to come to terms with them, to transform and build upon them, that keeps generating problems. They are impressions without expression, albeit not without effectivity.

Freud refers to expression as "abreaction" (SE 2: 9), mediated through action or through language as "a substitute for action" (SE 2: 8)—incidentally, the two factors that are the fulcra of Arendt's political philosophy and theory of natality.[1] The expression of trauma in action or language is a mitigated repetition (SE 2: 9) of the traumatizing cause, which does not permit the traumatic memory to linger on with the same force as before nor to garner still more strength outside the order of conscious psychic life. The non-symbolic languages and interactions of participants in an ecosystem are similarly deprived of the possibility of expressing ecological trauma, even though some (e.g., plants) deal better with radioactive isotopes or heavy metals by neutralizing them or adapting. In a countdown to ecosystems' collapse, it should be, therefore, possible to observe hysterical conversion phenomena, symptomatically appearing on the body of an ecosystem.

The analogy, which is by no means metaphoric, must be carefully calibrated. Freud and Breuer conclude that motor phenomena are the most frequent types of hysterical symptoms, when both channels of communicative expression and meaningful action are foreclosed. "The motor phenomena of hysterical attacks can be interpreted partly as universal forms of reaction appropriate to the affect accompanying the memory (such as kicking about and waving the arms and legs, which even young babies do), partly as a direct expression of these memories" (SE 2: 15). Movement of the body or of its parts in space is the hysterical substitute for language, itself a substitute for action. But movement is not reducible either to self-dislocation in space or to limb motions; growth is also a movement, on a slower timescale. When, within an ecosystem, unexpected growth takes place (whether in the positive/proliferating or negative/extinction-bound directions), it may be seen, at least in part, as an analogue of the "motor phenomena of hysterical attacks." Beyond this or that species deemed invasive or close to extinction, the growth-movement of this species on the body of the ecosystem it belongs (or, precisely, does not belong) to is a symptom. It supplants the interactions and communicative expressions that, in their biodiverse ensemble, make up an ecosystem. In the case of an invasive species, for instance, it "acts like a foreign body" within the body of an ecosystem not because it is brought from the outside, but because it induces a hysterical attack of ecosystemic magnitude.

Expression is a hinge between psychical and physiological registers, whereas (hysterical) conversion is a botched expression, letting elements from one register pass to the other without the mediations of language (not necessarily of a human variety) and action. The appropriate expression is context-, species-, age-, and body-specific, and its absence is more revealing about the functioning of psychical mechanisms than is the "normal" situation. This is Freud's rule of thumb—the principle of psychoanalysis, according to which the outlines of psychic life are understood on the basis of their psycho-pathologies, be they minor and innocuous or major and hugely disruptive. While I can offer here no more than a set of preliminary remarks on hysteric conversion and other disturbances in the ecological setting, it is crucial to keep to this principle: if an ecosystem has a mind, if it is an extended and extending mind or minds, as Aldo Leopold and Gregory Bateson argued in the middle of the past century, then it can suffer from mental problems that, in their turn, elucidate the "normal" functioning of ecosystemic minds.

In subsequent notes on psychotherapeutic approaches to hysteria, Freud connects the dots between hysteria and neurosis, suggesting that he "eventually found a way out of all these emerging doubts by the plan of treating all the other neuroses in question in the same way as hysteria" (SE 2: 257). This overarching "way out" had to do with the discovery that when it comes to "the *acquisition* of neuroses, their etiology is to be looked for in *sexual* factors" (SE 2: 257). Just as, applied to infants or prepubescent children, this Freudian affirmation was met with incredulity, so it may seem far-fetched to extend sexual factors to organisms that reproduce asexually or to entire ecosystems, with a mix of organic and inorganic components. Nevertheless, the sexual ontology of the world is acknowledged and celebrated in cosmovisions from the most diverse cultures; it was accepted also in the West from the Presocratics up until German Romanticism. Conceived as an embodied principle of aggregation, Eros is the red thread of attraction and sociality, traversing even inorganic beings, such as the rocks and the earth. In this broader field, the "*sexual* factors" behind neurosis (and, by extension, hysteria) are the undue physical, physiological, or enacted barriers to the free expression of sexuality.

Analysis and synthesis, segregation and aggregation (translated by Freud into the Greek categories of Thanatos and Eros), are the shared, transversal tendencies of physical and psychological realities, of material being and thinking, of religion and politics. Marked by psychosomatic and motor symptoms, "conversion" hysteria evinces with utmost clarity the co-belonging of physical (or physiological) and psychological processes. Freud's early terms for the hysterical-neurotic isolation of an unacceptable idea, which becomes "a nucleus and center of crystallization for the formation of a psychical group divorced from the ego" (SE 2: 123) or "the point at which a symptom has already broken through once" being "a weak spot at which it will break through again the next time" (SE 2: 264) testify to this co-belonging, or this continuum, of the psycho-physical dynamics of aggregation and disaggregation.

When ecological conditions are understood not as objective and measurable realities but as an embodied mind, or a conjunction of bodies-minds, then eco-hysteria may come to signify 1) the hysteria *of* ecology, and 2) the hysteric component of our relation to ecology. Freud's insights into the unconscious mechanisms of repression are indexed to specific maladies, including different kinds of hysteria. It would, therefore, be a propaedeutically and theoretically valuable exercise to map these mechanisms onto the two facets of eco-hysteria.

Before the formation of "*phobia proper*," anxiety hysteria deploys the technique of displacement "along a chain of connections" of fear or anxiety from its source to a substitute. The result, for instance, is "fear of a wolf, instead of a demand for love from the father" (SE 14: 155). The displacement following a chain of connections across species lines is already a good indication of the (potential, at least) involvement of other-than-human factors in hysterical symptomatology.

In *the anxiety hysteria of ecology*, displacements probably cross species boundaries even more frequently, but the chain of connections is symbiotic and biochemical, rather than symbolic-associative. Take defense mechanisms. If plants (say, corn seedlings) are under attack by caterpillars, they will emit biochemical volatile compounds to attract parasitic wasps, the predators of caterpillars.[2] Displacement takes the form of strategic alliance formation, but it would be wrong to assume that such defenses are perfectly algorithmically adjusted and rationally explicable. Whatever the strategy, it is also an acting out of anxiety. There is no plant consciousness without the plant unconscious. Vegetal unconscious is more diffuse than the plant cells and tissues deemed to be the calculating minds: it involves the surrounding air and the soil, in which plants' biochemical signature is deposited and which, at high concentrations, can be toxic to the very roots that released such exudates.[3] But hysterical displacement as such would entail the activation of defenses against harmless actors in the environmental drama, as well as excessive self-inhibition. These may include abnormal growth or the cessation of growth, as well as unwarranted physiological reactions (the release of exudates) that are tantamount to motor disturbances and other behavioral features of hysteria.

In *ecological anxiety hysteria*, we find a whole panoply of displacements of the fear of death. As the environment loses its automatically presupposed and rarely examined sense of life support (above all, of support for the species-life of *Homo sapiens*), it is diffracted into a contemplation of the concrete possibilities of dying. The initial displacement follows the trajectories of this diffraction: the fear of energy starvation and freezing to death in the case of the depletion of sources of fuel; the fear of drowning in flash floods and in the rising seas; the fear of lethal hunger due to the loss of fertile topsoils; the fear of suffocation in extreme smog; the fear of burning, or baking, alive in global heating. That mutually exclusive possibilities (e.g., freezing and boiling) are on a par in this complex of hysterical anxieties is indicative not only of their rooting in the unconscious, but also of the operations of the ecological mind itself, where the principle of non-contradiction does not hold sway. A further displacement to means of transport (for instance, passenger planes that account for a relatively small percentage of global CO_2 emissions) results in avoidance, self-prohibition, or self-inhibition (SE 14: 157), a paralysis of behaviors, such as traveling, mirroring in its objective outcome other, classical phobias, such as the fear of planes.

Conversion hysteria may be accompanied by the desaturation of affect from the symptom—in the words of Charcot, *"la belle indifférence des hystériques"*—or, the opposite, namely its condensation, in which a body part "has drawn the whole cathexis onto itself" (SE 14: 156). Freud mentions the role of regression in the "mechanism of conversion hysteria" (SE 14: 156), but we can only speculate on this role, given that the metapsychological paper on conversion hysteria has been lost. It seems likely that regression from symbolic expressions to bodily symptoms is at stake in the process Freud is hinting at, not to mention regression to other stages of psycho-sexual development centered on body parts that are physically or associatively close to the foci of these stages (the mouth, the anus)—while *"la belle indifférence"* would be a corollary of latency.

In *the conversion hysteria of ecology*, regression must unfold under the sign of the death drive, the striving of life to return to its prehistory—all the way to the inorganic existence whence it emerged. The loss of biodiversity and the non-linear trajectory of extinction are not merely the predetermined effects of objectively active and scientifically operationalizable causes; they are symptoms of ecological conversion hysteria in its regressive thrust. These symptoms appearing on the ecological body are utterly non-expressive, if they are attributable to purely external causes (changing average temperatures, falling humidity levels, etc.). Such an attribution itself, however, has a double meaning: it is *indicative of* the conversion hysteria of ecology and it *suffers from* an ecological conversion hysteria, insofar as it overlooks the deeper expressive connections between more-than-human minds and bodies.

In *ecological conversion hysteria*, there is also a regressive breakdown of the relation between symbolic expression and bodily symptoms: verbal expressions themselves become symptoms to be diagnosed on the cultural, political, civic bodies. "Speaking truth to power" at global climate gatherings à la Greta Thunberg; climate strikes; disruptions of concerts or damage to works displayed at galleries or museums; obsessions with "climate debt" all find their places within the hysteric breakdown. The avowed goal of these actions is to draw attention (to the problem, by drawing attention to themselves), so that even when speech is involved, it acts symptomatically in a way comparable to a displaced motor symptom. As Freud puts it: "In conversion hysteria the instinctual cathexis of the repressed idea is changed into the innervation of the symptom." Subsequently, and to varying extents, "the unconscious idea is drained empty by this discharge into innervation, so that it can relinquish its pressure upon the system Cs." (SE 14: 184). Although for all intents and purposes it seems that, in ecological conversion hysteria, desires are expressed (to stop using fossil fuels, to stop consuming animal flesh, to stop flying . . .), the negative form of these statements as well as their formulaic, performative, and repetitive enunciation betray their symptomatic nature. They are, to be sure, "innervated" by the "instinctual cathexis of the repressed idea," but this idea does not announce itself in the open. In the end, such actions often serve to "drain empty" the original sense of that which is repressed and to "relinquish its pressure upon the system," including the very system that is presented with the hysterical demand.

To take an obvious example, the concept of "climate strike" drains the idea and the desire behind a strike of their meaning. Workers' strikes have a clear target—the owners of the means of production—and set of demands: typically, higher wages in a usual strike; less often, the end of the capitalist system itself in a general strike.[4] A climate strike has neither a clear target nor a circumscribed set of demands nor, again, the potential to be transformed into a general strike. Paradoxically, the purely symbolic nature of such a strike coincides with its non-symbolic sense as a hysterical symptom on the civic-political body.

I

Inhibitions: of ecological thinking and/in action

One of the obstacles on the path to tackling the climate crisis is its amorphous, undelimited, total nature, in combination with a diluted sense of personal responsibility and of the capacity to do something meaningful about it. Both sober thinking and action are subject to inhibition in an individual and collective paralysis, which is of a piece with frantic attempts to do something, urgently, if without palpable effects.

As Freud observed in his 1926 text, inhibition is "intimately associated" with anxiety (SE 20: 87) and is detectable in the inability to perform a function. Anxiety and inhibition are caught up in a self-reinforcing loop: the more anxious one is, the more usual functioning is inhibited, and the more this functioning is inhibited, the greater the anxiety. Freud's example is that of the sexual function, which, when inhibited in men, amounts to impotence. Inhibition unfolds in several stages in this instance: "a turning away of the libido at the beginning of the process (psychical-unpleasure); an absence of the physical preparation for it (lack of erection); an abridgement of the sexual act (*ejaculatio praecox*) [...]; an arrest of the act before it has reached its natural conclusion (absence of ejaculation); or a non-appearance of the psychical outcome (lack of the feeling of pleasure in orgasm)" (SE 20: 88). How do these stages of inhibition apply to environmental action?

The first phase of dissuasion, the initial "turning away of the libido" from environmental action and even from thinking about the sources of the problem to be addressed, hinges on the immensity of the issue, of not knowing where to start. Libidinal divestment may take the form of sheer indifference ("if plants sprout afresh every spring, then why bother?") or that of extreme displeasure and distress provoked by everything associated with the climate crisis and with one's own inability to deal with this crisis ("if the problem is caused by generations upon generations of industrializing societies, then what can I do to change it?"). The process is either that of de-cathecting from the issue or of experiencing an exceptionally powerful negative cathexis.

Second, "the absence of physical preparation"—translated in male sexuality into a lack of erection—is, literally, the unpreparedness of political, social, and economic actors and agencies at national and international levels in the face immediate, rapidly multiplying environmental emergency situations (as illustrated, most recently, in the catastrophic floods that hit Valencia, Spain). It also refers to their inability to work for the long-term goal of mitigating the most extreme consequences of the climate crisis. This inhibition is not only psychic-affective but also psycho-somatic, indexed to the body and its organs, be it a biological body or a political one. So, the departments of forestry may wish to reduce the number and scope of wildfires, but they cannot do so without biodiverse forests, nor without adjusting to drier, hotter climates.

Third, "an abridgement of the sexual act" corresponds to quick-fix solutions proposed as though each of them were a magic key to addressing all climate woes. The uncompromising veganism of everyone in the world, the end of air travel, of nuclear energy, sexism, colonialism, and every other "single-issue" cause or effect are the abridgements of ecological thinking and action in a political *ejaculatio praecox*. To be sure, they overcome the early stages of inhibition—the diversion of libidinal energy and the absence of physical response—but they discontinue the process right after it has commenced, providing a shadow of satisfaction with a dogmatic and partial answer. These "abridgements" do just enough to keep inhibition in place: they yield a semblance of action, often wrapped in a mantle of self-righteousness heedless to any other arguments, in order to block out further thinking and to stop meaningful environmental action in its tracks. They fail to interrogate the deep historical, metaphysical, and psychological roots of the crisis, let alone to advocate for a systemic change beyond questions of personal and consumer responsibility, even and especially when *the* cause (such as capitalism or colonialism) is clearly identified.

Fourth, "an arrest of the act before it has reached its natural conclusion" is consistent with unending discussions around the Anthropocene and fossil fuels, cancerogenic pesticides and forever chemicals in food and in the environment, and even around increased global risks, chaos, unpredictability, tipping points, or mutually reinforcing factors in the planetary crisis. The ballooning industry of experts and consultants, the academic publication machine, international summits, and downgraded emission reduction goals—these are, by and large, inhibitions of effective solutions in the name of a persistent search for a solution. The infinite deferral they represent is the exact opposite of the precipitated programs of the political *ejaculatio praecox*. Both, however, are instances of inhibition, belonging to its different stages. The starkest difference between them has to do with time: the fast and the intolerably slow, abrupt termination and the interminable. In and of itself, acceleration or deceleration does not, for all that, manage to accomplish what it sets out to accomplish.

The final stage of inhibition is, properly speaking, supplemental, phantasmatic, or subjective. Everything has worked out as it should have, the act has been carried out to its conclusion, but the psychical outcome of pleasure has not been produced. Inhibition here circles back to the first stage, at which the rest of the stages have been obviated, namely libidinal divestment—a purely psychic process. Arguably, it is the fate of radical political and ecological programs to fall prey to this merciless blow of inhibition, where satisfaction with change is absent (especially after revolutionary euphoria dies out "the morning after" a revolution).[1] The same is true for the technocratic paradigm of crisis management, which privileges the urgent need of putting out the local fires of mushrooming emergencies over the task of contending with the root causes of the polycrisis.

The point is that, in Freud's theory and practice, inhibition is not synonymous with inaction. Only at the preliminary stage is this the case; in all others instances, inhibition *actively interferes with the act* and its psychological effects, while something is still happening under its oppressive cover. Furthermore, when it comes to motor activity, inhibition originating in "restrictions of the functions of the ego" (SE 20: 90) impairs the *functioning* of an organ (SE 20: 87), which refers to the organ's expected, usual function, rather than functionality *as such*, unless we are dealing with the "condition of general inhibition" (SE 20: 90). In all other circumstances, the inhibition of an expected function may actually give rise to other activations, recalling the earlier state of infantile polymorphous perversity. Could this be one of the reasons for the migration of ecological thinking and activism from the political couloirs to the space of contemporary art: museums, galleries, extra-academic art education, and alternative institutions?

Inhibition, then, is the self-restriction of the ego (more specific than repression and more closely connected to the motor function, motility, etc.) in an attempt "not to arouse the anxiety-symptom" (SE 20: 101). As a negative phenomenon, it calls for *less*—less involvement, action, engagement. Under the banner of neuroses, it is tightly bound to avoidances and phobias, as well as, culturally, taboos and self-restrictions that guarantee social coexistence. But, rather counterintuitively, the workings of inhibition veer on the side of excess, whether at the later stages of the inhibitory process or in the surprising activation of ego- and organ-functions that, in its positivity, generates symptoms, not least those that were meant to be obviated in the first place.

In a word, psychoanalytically speaking, the opposite of inhibition is not disinhibition! In response to the climate crisis, it is crucial to distinguish the ecological thinking and activism that are the positive *symptoms* of inhibition from those that are ways of *working through* the ideational, affective, politico-economic, and technological complexes that coalesce into an environmental catastrophe of planetary proportions. The gap separating them is narrow: it inheres in the apparent "waste of time" that is self-examination, occupied with the analysis of one's own motivations and cathexes, repressions and resistances.

In the course of his 1926 study, Freud puzzles over the pleasure derived *from* inhibition, including "certain sexual practices such as *coitus interruptus*, undischarged sexual excitation or enforced abstinence" (SE 20: 110). The desaturation of libidinal energy, which he had attributed to inhibition, clearly does not work in these instances. *Coitus interruptus* revels in the "arrest of the act before it has reached its natural conclusion"; it is the pleasure taken in non-completion, non-accomplishment, or the functionally improper accomplishment of the act. Instead of a foray into the territory beyond the pleasure principle (and the straightforwardly sadomasochist tendencies that traverse this territory), it signals a mutation of pleasure, whereby pleasure is derived from the frustration of pleasure, which always shadows inhibition.

Very often, academic (and even political) discussions thrive on an intellectual version of a perpetual *coitus interruptus*, particularly when dealing with the environmental crisis, among many other overlapping and mutually reinforcing crises. It remains to be seen whether, behind the scenes, this is the pleasure secretly taken in disaster and in the inevitability of fate heralding it (hence, inhibition would be *the* mechanism allowing for what could still be averted to become actually inevitable—and to draw tragic pleasure from impending doom), or whether this is the pleasure of unpleasure spawned by the inhibition itself and twisted into a positive phenomenon not only as far as its symptoms are concerned but also with respect to its psychical effects. Freud himself has no precise answer to the piquant twist of inhibition; "*non liquet*"— he writes—"it is not clear" (SE 20: 110).

Freud addresses sundry kinds of inhibition throughout his written body of work. In a late text, *An Outline of Psychoanalysis*, he mentions "developmental inhibitions" that "manifest themselves as the many sorts of disturbance in sexual life" (SE 23: 155). Here, development encompasses species-being and individual growth within the much-criticized, apparently teleological paradigm culminating in heterosexual genital-reproductive sexuality. In a more contingent key, development proceeds thanks to mutations, unforeseeable leaps, and catastrophic ruptures, as Freud himself acknowledges when he links stages in psychosexual development to the history of life on earth and, more broadly still, to geological epochs (the long period of latency, for instance, memorializing the latency of life itself during the Ice Age, or, in more modest biological terms, the dormancy of a seed or of trees in the northern hemisphere's winter). Consequently, the inhibitions of ecological thinking and acting at the time of crisis amount to the developmental inhibitions of humanity as a species, not in the sense of its incapacity to be transformed into another, posthuman form of life, but in the sense of cultivating an alternative civilizational relation to the environment. These inhibitions themselves are bound to be manifest as disturbances, amplifying those that irrupt in a crisis.

Another sort of inhibition is related to waking and sleeping states. In sleep, Freud avers, with an eye to Aristotle's influential essay on the subject, a non-relation to the external world results in the withdrawal of cathexes from sense organs. "Since the waking ego governs motility, that function is paralyzed in sleep, and accordingly a good part of the inhibitions imposed on the unconscious become superfluous. The withdrawal or reduction of these 'anticathexes' thus allows the id what is now a harmless amount of freedom" (SE 23: 166). Inhibitions are removed when no action is expected—for instance, in sleep—and freedom is harmless because it has no palpable effects in actuality. Prevalent academic treatments of the eco-crisis are *either* fixated at the stage of inhibition where acts are arrested (this is, more generally, the psychoanalytic background for the divorce of theory from practice) *or* take place as though in sleep, where the removal of inhibition affords "a harmless amount of freedom," given that the motility function is "paralyzed," and the relation to the external world is suspended. By contrast, in sleepwalking, this function is not disabled, but it is not governed by the ego, which is what can happen when the removal of inhibitions does not coincide with a return to one's senses, so to speak. Sleepwalking toward a disaster, in this very precise formulation, is wrapped in plenty of dreamy theory that remains unintegrated with practice.

Freud analyzes the "inhibitions of work" in the little-commented case of "demonological neurosis" that afflicted seventeenth-century painter Christoph Haizmann. Upon the death of his father, Haizmann suffered "from melancholic depression, with an inhibition in his work and (justified) fears about his future" (SE 19: 80). He then signed a pact with the devil (twice) in order to regain a father substitute and, consequently, his "capacity to work" (SE 19: 82).

Inhibitions of work come closest to the paralysis of practice, and the question is at what price (also the price as set within psychic economy) these blockages may be overcome. On whose terms will inaction in the face of the climate crisis come to an end? Who will be the father substitute, sanctioning activity? The promoters of the Green New Deal, in which the father figure is still none other than capital?

Intriguingly, in his other texts, such as *Beyond the Pleasure Principle*, Freud considers the devil to be a personification of the unconscious and of the forbidden desires populating it. As such, the devil is, indeed, an agent of disinhibition, but he cannot be a father figure, an authority linked to the superego. The source of inhibition is similarly uncertain: it may be anxiety or melancholia, on the one hand, or the denial of masturbatory pleasure, on the other. In a short diary note from August 3, 1938, Freud writes: "The ultimate ground of all intellectual inhibitions and all inhibitions of work seems to be the inhibition of masturbation in childhood. But perhaps it goes deeper; perhaps it is not its inhibition by external influences but its unsatisfying nature in itself. There is always something lacking for complete discharge and satisfaction [...]" (SE 23: 300).

As he invokes "all intellectual inhibitions and all inhibitions of work," Freud combines theory and practice, linking the arrest of both to the external prohibition of masturbation in childhood and to the internal logic of masturbation with its unsatisfactory outcomes. The final two stages of the inhibition of the male sexual function, which Freud described in his 1926 work, match the self-inhibiting nature of masturbation. According to the logic of the phenomenon, however, self-inhibition translates into *more*, rather than *less*, of the same in the elusive quest for "complete discharge and satisfaction." A proliferation of *fin de siècle* discourses around global ecosystems' collapse *and* the profession of newfound love for the planet and all its species belong to the same affective-theoretical disavowal of the end, or to inhibition in its external and internal aspects. Extreme urgency to act *now* and the snowballing of ecological publications, events, summits, workshops (sometimes sliding toward the New Age terrain of wellness and self-help) bespeak the prohibition of masturbation and masturbatory frustration. Inhibition is, therefore, the foremost issue to be tackled in the prevalent responses and non-responses to the environmental crisis.

J

Jokes and their relation to the eco-crisis

Let's begin with a joke:

"You know global warming is real when . . .
-you can say *110 degrees* without fainting;
-you realize asphalt has a liquid state;
-a rancher tells you that he wishes it would rain, not for himself because he's seen it, but for his 7-year-old;
-you go to McDonald's to get coffee and pour it on your lap—just to cool off!"

This joke and the chapter of the book in which it is included are likely to be met with an objection that it is highly inappropriate to laugh about the climate crisis. Doesn't a humorous approach deflate the existential significance of the global disaster in the making? Isn't it likely to pass the issue off as a mere laughing matter, eroding mobilization at all levels of society to act in order to fight against, or at least to mitigate, the crisis?

In fact, jokes largely work *because* they are inappropriate, that is to say, because they touch upon materials generally confined to the unconscious and jealously guarded by the forces of repression. They are the oblique expressions of the drives—of the life instinct as much as of the death drive—which is why, since his early research on the "psychopathologies of everyday life," Freud groups them together with slips of tongue and dreams as inroads into the unconscious. The same mechanisms are operative in jokes as in these other inadvertent disclosures of unconscious contents: "condensation, displacement, indirect representation" (SE 8: 95) or "an *allusion* to the repressed element, like a representation of it in indirect speech" (SE 11: 30). So, if we sincerely wish to hear what the unconscious tells us about the eco-crisis, we should listen carefully to the jokes dealing with this issue.

To return to the opening salvo of this chapter, the conflation of actual heat and global warming is one of the reasons why the joke works, and, as always, there is a large grain of truth in it. In everyday conversations, this conflation (treating weather and climate interchangeably) is rampant, making it a part of *social* reality. Politicians who deny the reality of climate change do so publicly and with comically great aplomb. The "real" of global warming ("You know global warming is real when . . .") is, therefore, conveyed through what it is *not*, through what is much more accessible to the senses than complex chains of causality, feedback loops, statistical measurements, and probabilistic models.

The joke further speaks to the need to have concrete, palpable evidence of global warming and the obverse, the lack of such evidence, where it is ultimately subject to belief and to a nearly religious distinction between having and not having faith. The paradox is that direct, empirical evidence will always point to the weather, not to the climate—hence, all the hyperbolic assertions the joke marshals. Within the strictly empirical sphere of evidence, climate change denial always wins: it is always easy to dismiss extreme weather as a one-off phenomenon, not as part of a worrisome climate trend. And yet, our joke also points beyond disparate pieces of hyperbolic empirical evidence to *habituation*, to getting used to something unthinkable before (like saying and experiencing 110 degrees Fahrenheit with reference to outside temperature) due to its frequent repetition. A similar thread of habituation and perdurance is detectable in the contrary effects of a hot beverage in an even hotter environment and a 7-year-old's experiential unfamiliarity with rain.

How is the joke related to the drives and their repression? What we intuit through it is life in an unlivable world, an absurd continuation of existence where you tread on asphalt in a liquid state and cool down by pouring hot coffee on yourself. (Actually, the technique of cooling down by sweating as a result of drinking hot beverages, such as tea, is not uncommon in the countries of Central Asia and in China.) The joke *disavows* the death drive (more positively put, it affirms life despite its impossibility in extreme climate conditions), and it does so by *fetishizing* global warming and its hyperbolic reality. As a result, it generates substitute pleasure, which is otherwise prohibited when we related to the climate crisis with all due seriousness. For, in line with Freud's "jokes book," joking is "an activity which aims at deriving pleasure from mental processes, whether intellectual or otherwise" (SE 8: 96).

Analyzing climate, global warming, and eco-crisis jokes, we gain privileged access to the territory where unconscious relations to these unfolds. Such jokes do not always indulge in disavowal; rather, they may embrace the death drive and laugh at its aftereffects. Consider the following joke:

> "Two planets meet. The first one asks, 'How are you?' 'Not so well,' the second answers, 'I've got the *Homo sapiens*.' 'Don't worry,' the other replies, 'I had the same. That won't last long.'"

The pleasure this joke generates hails from beyond the pleasure principle. In a masochistic inversion, one takes comfort in the return of human life to the inorganic condition—to death—and, concomitantly, in the continuation of planetary existence after the extinction of the human species. *Homo sapiens* doubles here as the name of a disease, from which the planet suffers. The consolation is that, on the scales of deep geological and astronomical time, this disease is not a long-lasting one: the species comes and goes in a cosmic instant. The joke belongs, then, in the genre of phantasies about "the world without us," represented as a much healthier place after humankind goes extinct. If such a mode of imagining is at its core nihilistic, it is because it proceeds along the tracks of the death drive, where "pleasure beyond pleasure" is achieved through the imagined and desired dissolution of all tensions.

We do not need to go into Freud's classification of jokes as "innocent" or "tendentious," "obscene" or "hostile." Their differences boil down to the deeper or more superficial layers of pleasure (hence, of the unconscious) which various types of jokes may access and activate—both acknowledging and transgressing the internalized social prohibition to experience pleasure (SE 8: 103). One feature of the "technique of jokes" stands out, however: the "employment of sophistry for the disguised representation of the truth" (SE 8: 107–8). Assuming that one wishes to speak to the unconscious (and to listen to it, of course), this is a better technique than the currently fetishized fact-checking or "science-based" PR. Updated for the twenty-first century, Freud does not endorse immersion in alternative facts or drowning in the ocean of post-truth; rather, his advice reveals how post-truth may be read as a symptom and how a symptomatic or symptomal treatment of the eco-crisis through the technique of jokes may be effective. In the case of our first joke, hyperbole and the conflation of climate and weather do the trick; in the second joke, inversion and the voice of planetary thinking do so.

In other cases, climate jokes may be directly sexualized, tapping straight into libidinal resources. For example:

"If you meet a woman, start talking about global warming. It's a real icebreaker."

The linchpin of the joke is the merging of the literal and figurative senses of "icebreaking," pointing still further in the direction of frigidity and overcoming it, along with other effects of extreme repression. Sexually speaking, icebreaking is symbolic of a penetrative practice, where the crucial distinction is between a forced breaking of ice (as by specialized ships) and its cracking and melting as a result of thawing. But the naïve, albeit crucial, question in this regard is: What makes global warming and the climate crisis sexy? Why is it supposed to spark an intimate relation? And what is the attractiveness, invariably sublimating sexuality, in endlessly "talking about" it in broader public contexts?

In a 1910 letter to Friedrich S. Krauss, the editor of the periodical *Anthropophyteia*, Freud reflects on erotic jokes. These jokes, he notes, "give us direct information as to which of the component instincts of sexuality are retained in a given group of people as particularly efficient in producing pleasure" (SE 11: 233). He goes on to define the most delicious among these *complexive jokes*, which "owe their exhilarating and cheerful effect to the ingenious uncovering of what are, as a rule, repressed complexes" (SE 11: 234).

Erotic climate jokes shed light on the knot, in which the two seemingly opposed drives, Eros and Thanatos, life and death instincts, are tied together. This, too, pertains to the domain of sadomasochism (as, indeed, do a vast majority of eco-crisis and climate jokes), but the nexus of the two instincts ends up being highly volatile and indeterminate: *either* the erotic content of such jokes wells up by way of resistance to the dissolution signaled by the death drive *or* it is affirmed together, in resonance with this drive. Plus, since the unconscious will have none of the principle of non-contradiction, a third option should be added, namely the simultaneous affirmation of the life and death instincts *via* the resistance the former offers to the latter. After all, the erotic aggregation and increase in complexity animated by the pleasure principle are punctuated by fleeting instants of satisfaction that are the pale reflections of what lies beyond this same principle (the dissolution of vital tensions in death as *permanent* satisfaction). Don't erotic climate jokes indulge in something similar, mixing the two drives?

The purest distillation of the mix is evident in the following joke:

"Putin's love for humankind heats up the planet by 2.35 degrees annually—a phenomenon also known as global warming."

Love and death converge around heat, which may be life-giving or mortiferous and which becomes *both* on the terms of the joke. The abandonment of energy transition targets as a result (but also on the pretext) of the war of aggression Russia has waged on Ukraine is one way to interpret this pithy saying. Another is the "business as usual" model, according to which dependence on Russian natural gas and oil put the brakes on Europe's and other regions' energy transition. Again, otherwise incompatible practices lead to the same outcome and conjure up the same cause: Putin's death-bearing "love for humankind." And, since we are on the subject of Russia's full-scale invasion of Ukraine, it is also worth recalling the mass orgy that was planned on the outskirts of Kyiv in the expectation of an impending nuclear holocaust or crushing defeat in the war during its early days in 2022. Here, too, life and death instincts united in a resistant affirmation or in affirmative resistance of the one to the other.

To Freud, jokes convey the impossibility of a total renunciation of desire. "What these jokes whisper may be said aloud: that the wishes and desires of men have a right to make themselves acceptable alongside of exacting and ruthless morality" (SE 8: 110). All too often, climate activism steps in as a representative of such morality, demanding big personal sacrifices and renunciation. Climate and eco-crisis jokes reassert the right of "wishes and desires" in the face of renunciation; they are the harbingers of a desire which does not disappear but is simply repressed, pent up, and forced to burst in the least expected forms.

Given the nature of the subject, on the topic of global warming, the "skeptical" type of jokes are the most common ones—and here we come back to the beginning of our discussion. However, skepticism is not limited to doubting the findings of climate science; it goes to the heart of the question of truth. To illustrate the point, Freud himself recounts the joke about a Jew traveling to Cracow: "Two Jews met in a railway carriage at a station in Galicia. 'Where are you going?' asked one. 'To Cracow', was the answer. 'What a liar you are!' broke out the other. 'If you say you're going to Cracow, you want me to believe you're going to Lemberg. But I know that in fact you're going to Cracow. So why are you lying to me?'" (SE 11: 115). The technique of absurdity in this joke is the "assertion of the first Jew," according to which "the second is lying when he tells the truth and is telling the truth by means of a lie." "Is it the truth," Freud goes on to ask, "if we describe things as they are without troubling to consider how our hearer will understand what we say? Or is this only jesuitical truth, and does not genuine truth consist in taking the hearer into account and giving him a faithful picture of our own knowledge?" (SE 11: 115).

Is it not the same with climate skeptics? In other words, is it the truth if one communicates climate change "without troubling to consider how" they will understand it? Are such audiences ever taken into account and given "a faithful picture of our own knowledge"? With appeals to the institution of science, let alone the practice of fact-checking, one is asked to bow to the sheer authority of the institution and of a fact apparently not open to discordant interpretations. These are appeals to *believe* that mask, if not outright deny, their anchoring in structures of faith, as well as the irreducibility of empirical evidence to the *reality* of climate change (recall the wording: "You know climate change is *real* . . ."). They are attempts to instill credulity and absolutize the authority it both entails and buttresses, without the foundational transformations of love (SE 7: 150). So, instead of focusing exclusively on the incontrovertible evidence of climate change, it is necessary to work on "genuine truth," which Freud exemplifies through the joke. Another joke, more self-depreciating than the one about the Jew going to Cracow, may be a good start:

"This text was made of 100% biodegradable, recycled words."

K

Kissing and knowing

In the final chapter of my book on St. Hildegard of Bingen, I have outlined a form of ecological knowing that learns from kissing, rather than biting into, digesting, and assimilating what is to be known.[1] With subtle indications from Hildegard's texts, I have interpreted the mystical kiss in its full ecological scope, including contacts among various elemental domains, the brushing of living surfaces (be they vegetal, animal, or human), the operations of the senses receiving the kiss of the word, sound, sight, and so forth. Nevertheless, to flesh out the model of ecological knowing predicated on the kiss, we must resort to the insights of psychoanalysis and the modifications of sexuality that play themselves out in this outward expression of love.

In *Three Essays on Sexuality*, Freud proposes the emergence of "the instinct for knowledge" from the "sexual researches of childhood." He is careful to specify that "this instinct cannot be counted among the elementary instinctual components, nor can it be classed as exclusively belonging to sexuality. Its activity corresponds on the one hand to a sublimated manner of obtaining mastery, while on the other hand it makes use of the energy of scopophilia" (SE 7: 194). Already Freud's depiction of the activity of knowing lays a heavy emphasis on the separation of the knower from the known (in obtaining mastery and, above all, in scopophilia, which privileges the visual relation). Conversely, the other materialist theory of knowing, more or less explicitly spelled out in philosophy from Augustine to Hegel and on to Nietzsche and Derrida, has to do with the digestion and assimilation of the known in the knower, doing away with the separation between them.

A common source of such materialist theories is the philosophy of Aristotle, where *to threptikon* (usually translated as "nutritive soul") is the basic principle of vitality, shared by plants, animals, and humans. At times, Aristotle attributes only one function—to obtain nutrition—to this principle; at other times, he lists the nutritive and reproductive functions together under the same heading. There are precise reasons for this apparent conflation: in plants, where *to threptikon* initially comes into being, the two functions are closely related (at least, if one brackets sexual reproduction). The point is that, for Aristotle, reproduction is invariably derivative from nutrition, whereas, for Freud, sexuality charges with its energy nutritive activities as well, since the very first stage of psycho-sexual development is oral (and the second is anal).

The physical-anatomic convergence of nutritive and sexual activities on the same organs is the underlying subject of dialectical and psychoanalytic reflections in Hegel and Freud alike. In Hegelian dialectics, the investment of the same organ (here: the mouth) with the highest and the lowest functions (e.g., speaking and eating/spitting) is taken as a sign of the speculative identity of opposites that receive their meaning from their belonging together. So do the corresponding experiences of inspiration and disgust. Freud, for his part, is aware that the mouth is the first point of entry of food as much as the epicenter of the oral stage of sexual development, which cannot help but color one's affective relation to nourishment. Its exercise of mastery depends on biting into and shredding the nourishing other to bits, while "scopophilic energy" is quelled (the reduction of distance makes it impossible to overview the object, which is interiorized). Now, the lips with their capacity for kissing and sucking prevent a violent destruction of the nourishing and/or beloved other—not least because they are activated before the infant has any teeth. A different knowledge instinct suggests itself here.

Freud invokes the arbitrariness of the line separating normalcy from perversion in kissing and the equally arbitrary nature of the corollary attitude of disgust: "The use of the mouth as a sexual organ is regarded as a perversion if the lips (or tongue) of one person are brought into contact with the genitals of another, but not if the mucous membranes of the lips of both of them come together. This exception is the point of contact with what is normal" (SE 7: 151). On the other side of the exception lies disgust. Freud proceeds to make fun of the arbitrariness of such normalcy taken literally: "a man who will kiss a pretty girl's lips passionately, may perhaps be disgusted at the idea of using her tooth-brush, though there are no grounds for supposing that his own oral cavity, for which he feels no disgust, is any cleaner than the girl's" (SE 7: 151–2). The explanation for this self-contradictory behavior is the "libidinal over-valuation of the sexual object," bordering on idealization.

A kiss, lingering at the oral stage of sexuality, is the stamp of "libidinal over-valuation," which takes care not to destroy the sexual object, but to enter into a mutual relation with it, the relation devoid of mastery and scopophilia, one that lacks an inherent moment of satisfaction, unlike the sense of being sated in the course of digestion. Through a kiss, one receives the other without assimilating and without destroying the other's alterity. A non-destructive and non-extractive knowing, it is also a psycho-sexual foundation of non-extractive ontology, where the world as such is libidinally over-valued, regardless of the disgust, which many of its material aspects may incite.[2] Kissing is knowing otherwise, also on psychoanalytic grounds.

As he develops the motif of the lips in *Three Essays*, Freud notes that "the child's lips, in our view, behave like an erotogenic zone, and no doubt stimulation by the warm flow of milk is the cause of the pleasurable sensation" (SE 7: 181). "If that significance [of the labial region] persists," he adds, "these same children when they are grown up will become epicures in kissing, will be inclined to perverse kissing, or, if males, will have a powerful motive for drinking and smoking. If, however, repression ensues, they will feel disgust at food and will produce hysterical vomiting. The repression extends to the nutritional instinct owing to the dual purpose served by the labial zone" (SE 7: 182).

"The warm flow of milk" as a source of pleasure is exemplary, or synecdochic, of pleasure decoupled from a necessary satisfaction: it rejoices in the experience while experiencing it, without an inherent limit. Any non-instrumental pleasure harkens back to this structure: feeling one's skin kissed by light wind or water, relating to artworks, reading (not to amass knowledge but to be touched and excited by the text, of a book or of the world). But, although lips are at the forefront of both activities, sucking and kissing—between which Freud does not make a conceptual differentiation—have distinct rhythms, the lightness or heaviness of touch, the goal of brushing upon the other or extracting something from them. (These two can lapse into a zone of indistinction when deeper parts of the oral cavity are involved in kissing.) Even if the "original" instrumental purpose of infant sucking is to extract "the warm flow of milk," the pleasure that both motivates and is produced in the course of the act is in excess of that purpose, providing it with a temporal and affective horizon, putting it in its place, radically contextualizing it. When this pleasure is untethered to extractive pursuits, it yields another paradigm of knowing (tactile, intimate, moist).

At the same time, the knowing that resides in a kiss has an underside, notably the negativity of rejecting the competing epistemic model. Opposition to extraction, the refusal of incorporation, is the hysterical position, as Freud has it, largely motivated by the repression of the disgust that awakens at the thought or sight of mucous contact. Vehement anti-extractivism in the fields of energy generation and knowing as a whole may be a case of this position, a counter-position, or an op-position determined, by and large, by the forces of repression. Technically speaking, the sense of disgust prevails over pleasure when the dual purpose of the same organ and, thus, the speculative dialectical charge it contains are intolerable. The victory of disgust and unbridled negativity are traces of a failed idealization, when the libidinal overvaluation of the object is not there. Political environmental action and alternative models of knowing must guard against the equivalents of hysterical vomiting of the system.

In *Introductory Lectures on Psychoanalysis*, Freud returns to the question of perversion in kissing. From the standpoint of genital sexuality, the gathering of the sexual impulse in any other area of the body is perverse. "Even a kiss can claim to be described as a perverse act," Freud contends, "since it consists in the bringing together of two oral erotogenic zones instead of the two genitals. Yet no one rejects it as perverse; on the contrary, it is permitted in theatrical performances as a softened hint at the sexual act. But precisely kissing can easily turn into a complete perversion—if, that is to say, it becomes so intense that a genital discharge and orgasm follow upon it directly, an event that is far from rare" (SE 16: 322).

The kiss twists free of normative, reproductive sexuality, shaking off its purpose-driven, teleological structure. The knowledges a kiss stimulates are, likewise, not reproductive—a reproductive system of knowing is the mainstay of ideology, even if it is called "science"—but contact-driven, based on exposure and sharing, rather than assimilation and appropriation. Being non-reproductive, such knowing is singular, finite, unrepeatable. Every kiss is mystical from the extractivist perspective: in its simultaneous intimacy and breadth of scope the kiss extends as far as the elements, overflowing the limits of teleological knowledge. Its positive non-accomplishment may even derail (unexpectedly, spontaneously) steady progress toward the achievement of an instrumentally posed goal, as in the "complete perversion" that kissing represents, bringing the normatively framed sexual relation to a premature end. The kiss then shatters teleology and muddles its relation to time, or, more precisely, brings time back into the equation, signaling the event that irrupts in and disturbs a predetermined sequence of occurrences.

The knowledges born from a kiss, then, are perverse knowledges, but they are perverse within a framework that perverts the heterogeneity of time, disrespects the porosity of physical and psychic boundaries-membranes, and dismisses the essential superficiality of contact-touch (which is, for Aristotle, in the same position vis-à-vis all the other senses as *to threptikon* is vis-à-vis other capacities and vital principles of the psyche, notably that of a ceaselessly heaving, mutating, forming, deforming, and transforming ground). Psychoanalytic knowledge, too, rebels against this perverse framework, despite its aspiration to be regarded as a respectable science. It is in this sense that Freud breaks the ironclad and exclusive association of the sexual and the genital, showing that it is not "only a question of the genital organs versus the other organs." "What are you going to do," he asks himself in a dialogic style he sometimes experiments with in his works, "about the numerous experiences which show you that the genitals can be represented as regards their yield of pleasure by other organs, as in the case of kissing or the perverse practices of voluptuaries or of the symptoms of hysteria?" (SE 16: 324). In kissing, the genitals are represented by the lips, and it is not at all guaranteed that such representation, whether deemed perverse or normal, does not also operate on the side of the object—who very often is another subject. If the organs of kissing stand in for other organs in view of their effects ("their yield of pleasure"), why couldn't the kissed also stand in for anything or anyone in the world? This way, the epistemology of kissing is launched into its fully ecological orbit.

When Freud discusses the infantile theories of the origin of babies, he, perhaps inadvertently, reinscribes the kiss in the logic of reproductive sexuality. "Thus," he observes, "for instance, there is the significant theory that a baby is got by a kiss—a theory which obviously betrays the predominance of the erotogenic zone of the mouth" (SE 9: 223). The close bond between the two aspects of the Aristotelian *to threptikon*—nourishment and reproduction—appears in these early researches, in which children, "following the lead of the impulses of their own sexuality form theories of babies originating from eating, of their being born through the bowels, and of the obscure part played by the father" (SE 11: 79).

Nonetheless, at the oral stage, there is a bifurcation, which has to do with ingestion or non-ingestion through the mouth, where the latter does not necessarily connote the frustration of desire. A kiss is the moment of non-ingestion, by contrast to eating. To view a kiss as productive or reproductive is not the same as viewing the act of swallowing and then excreting something or someone along analogous lines. The "significant theory" of birth through a kiss (also promulgated in Christian theology by the likes of St. Bernard of Clairvaux in connection to the birth of Jesus), which Freud cites, is fundamentally different from that of a birth (and knowledge) through ingestion, replete with unmistakably violent overtones—"by that time [when they formulate the latter theory, MM], they already have a notion of the sexual act, which appears to them to be something hostile and violent" (SE 11: 79). The refusal to eat is only partly attributable to the repression of oral sexuality; on its positive side, it reconnects to the orality of a kiss, where the other—indeed, much of the world—is not eaten up and where a drastically different relation to knowing is silently announced.

L

Libidinal ecologies

Since his earliest, pre-psychoanalytic investigations, Freud presented a model of the psyche in economic terms. But that was only half the story, as Freud himself recognized. For instance, in the 1924 work, *An Autobiographical Study*, he comprehended his metapsychology as "a method of approach according to which every mental process is considered in relation to three co-ordinates, which I described as *dynamic, topographical*, and *economic* respectively" (SE 20: 58–9). The topographical coordinates of mental processes evoke, contra Descartes, a spatial model of the mind: they lend to it not only extension, but also a shape and depth that are absent from the economic framework. Note that these are *not* metaphors but modes of psychic self-organization and distribution. What happens then with libidinal fluxes and their blockages on the rugged terrain of psychic life, hosting the equivalents of rivers and underground aquifers? Is there a *libidinal ecology* implicit in Freud's writings alongside the overemphasized *libidinal economy*?

As always, it is advisable to start with disruptions and failures, those instances where libidinal ecologies are troubled. In *Introductory Lectures on Psychoanalysis*, as well as in the late essay, "Analysis Terminable and Interminable," Freud addresses the "fixations of the libido." This is a more complete, and apparently more formal, way of naming fixations, referring to the blockages of libidinal flows or their channeling to surprising objects. So, a foot fetish is a fixation of the libido, which is excessive and premature, a mechanism also "indispensable for the causation of neuroses" (SE 16: 348–9). Fixation is a variation on the theme of object choice, which, according to the economic model, represents a libidinal "investment," a cathexis binding libidinal energy, rather than letting it circulate freely. In the topographic (and the ecological) model, however, instead of investments, fixations and object choice in general are seen as shaping desire—that is, as the concretization of desire in determinate formations. The problem of fixation is, precisely, rigidity—the immutability and the impassability of the shape that is produced. The difference between the economic and the ecological approaches is already glaring here: only in the latter do cathexes, be they fixations or more "normal" object choices, form the landscapes (and the riverscapes) of psychic life.

The economy of the libido is closely tied to Freud's earliest project of scientific psychology, which, though he eventually abandoned it, continued to inform many of his subsequent approaches, including at the level of metapsychology. It is no wonder, then, that aspects of the energy paradigm from the discipline of physics percolate into the economic model. When he refers to subjects with a "special 'adhesiveness of the libido,'" Freud comments that their treatment is typically slow "because, apparently, they cannot make up their minds to detach libidinal cathexes from one object and displace them on to another, although we can discover no special reason for this cathectic loyalty" (SE 23: 241). Freud detects in this attitude what he calls "psychical inertia," the deceleration of cathexes in keeping with the kinds of explanations one encounters in physics. What is particularly important, however, is that the implicit equivalences of libidinal cathexes allowing for displacement and subsequent transference in therapeutic settings are embedded in a scientific-economic paradigm, which operates with indifferent quanta of energy. Their abstract framing (including by some analysands, said to be less prone to psychical inertia) enables their relative disembeddedness and mobility. Conversely, libidinal ecologies render detachment, displacement, and transference more difficult because they treat as constitutive the unique context and singularity of relational knots tied in psychic life. Here, strict equivalences become all but impossible. The difference, which Freud pinpointed, between psychically inert and psychically mobile patients, may be indicative of the predominance of libidinal ecologies in some and of libidinal economies in others among the analysands.

Change and ostensible stagnation acquire distinct senses in libidinal ecologies and economies, as do psychoanalytic practices themselves. When Freud writes that "in another group of cases we are surprised by an attitude in our patients which can only be put down to a depletion of the plasticity, the capacity for change and further development, which we should ordinarily expect" (SE 23: 241), is he alluding to the ecologies of the libido, where plasticity and development are triggered by environmental interactions? But where these are stymied, changes may still take place in a rapid divestment of libidinal energies and their equally rapid investment into a new object, according to the economic model of the psyche. In other words, "psychical inertia" (SE 23: 242) may be consistent with the less evident, slower, and more durable development, rather than with sheer stagnation. The meaning of *dynamic* is thus altered, depending on its insertion into the economic or the topographic context of mental processes, where topography is not a practice of mapping the surfaces and depths of psychic strata but a conglomeration of relations, which lends it an ecological feel.

Libidinal economies are frames of mind, where investment into the love object yields the return of satisfaction or the non-return of "insufficient satisfaction," as Freud puts it in one of the first texts to mention sexual libido, defining it as "*psychical desire*" (SE 3: 107). Even if unconscious, the subject is the one who is at the helm of such psychic operations. In libidinal ecologies, conversely, desire is triggered, often by an unidentifiable combination of external factors. In effect, the initial passivity of the subject of desire vis-à-vis its object is also typical of the economic approach, but there it is the zero point of psychic investment into this or that object, rather than another one. On the one hand, the lack of mastery (and especially of self-mastery) by the unconscious subject in these situations invariably reverts back to trauma in the economic mindset: in the 1896 text on "the neuro-psychoses of defense," for instance, Freud cites the case of a boy who "had been abused by someone of the female sex, so that his libido was prematurely aroused, and then, a few years later, he had committed an act of sexual aggression against his sister, in which he repeated precisely the same procedures to which he himself had been subjected" (SE 3: 164–5). On the other hand, in libidinal ecologies, the arousing calls from others are received throughout the body, across its multiple, distracted, anarchic sites of awakening that need not be obscurely registered as traumatic.

The terms I am using to portray libidinal ecologies are not chosen on a whim; Freud helps himself to them in the course of sketching out the outlines of pre-genital sexualities. His elaboration of "the development of the libido" in *Introductory Lectures on Psychoanalysis* refers to the emergence of genital sexuality as a "turning-point" to which all other strivings of the sexual instinct are subordinated. "This is preceded," he continues, "by a sexual life that might be described as distracted—the independent activity of the different component instincts striving for organ-pleasure. This anarchy is mitigated by the abortive beginnings of 'pregenital' organizations" (SE 16: 328). The predominance of certain organs (the mouth, the anus) at the earlier stages of libidinal development is not on a par with the subordination of all components of the sexual instinct to the genitals; these other organs mitigate anarchy, but do not do away with it. Distraction is the striving of the libido in many directions at once, seeking pleasure from everything and everyone, and at any site, with every organ. It is the name for heeding the call of the other, answered throughout the bodily extension with each organ semi-independently "striving for organ-pleasure." The libidinal ecologies that unfold in such distracted, anarchic, plural tendencies follow the lead of vegetal life, which develops in the manner of the libido prior to the centralization of the genital stage (or, more precisely, it is the libido prior to centralization that develops in a vegetal manner—and it is by no means certain that the earliest anarchy is ever fully superseded).

With the lingo of "portfolio diversification" currently in vogue, it may seem as though investments can absorb the plurality of strivings in pre-genital sexuality. Nonetheless, diversification is not the same as distraction, which betokens an excess of attention or an unconscious hyperattention, no longer fitting within the limits of a purpose-oriented, investment-driven endeavor, bent on maximizing its returns. There is no coherent investment strategy here—just a forever incomplete, but positively instigating in its incompleteness, effort to respond and to correspond to the call of the other, libidinally resonating in pleasures, touches, and flows of instinct. Perhaps libidinal ecology starts resembling Bataille's general economy, where squandering and excess are key, and with good reason, seeing that general economy is, at bottom, an ecology.[1] The point is that, extrapolating from Freud, the libido develops in an ecological vein until the very last "stage" ("the turning-point") of genital sexuality, when it adopts an economic model of psychic life. A plethora of historically relevant reasons may be cited for this understanding (and self-understanding) of the psyche. On its own terms, however, the language of investment and the entire economic paradigm are not appropriate to libidinal development prior to that turning point.

Freud's candor in *An Outline of Psychoanalysis* leads us to supplement the anarchic, distracted, plural, topographic, and essentially relational ontological descriptors of libidinal ecologies with an epistemic qualification: virtually unknowable. "It is hard to say anything of the behavior of the libido in the id and in the superego," he admits. "All that we know about it relates to the ego, in which at first the whole available quota of libido is stored up. We call this state absolute, primary *narcissism* [. . .] Throughout the whole of life the ego remains the great reservoir from which libidinal cathexes are sent out to objects and into which they are also once more withdrawn" (SE 23: 150). From this admission, we may infer that the division between conscious processes and the unconscious is behind the distinction between libidinal economies and ecologies, respectively, and it is a division that makes itself *known* exclusively in the conscious life of the ego. In fact, the ego accumulates (stores up) libidinal energy and draws on the libido as a "great reservoir" to cathect parts of it to objects or to withdraw such investments. Primary narcissism is the cradle and the grave of libidinal economy, whereas the behavior of the libido in the unconscious likely does not obey the same rules of the game in the absence of the egoic subject *or* when the ego is recast as an eco-subject, an interface lacking the interiority of a reserve.

Granted: "it is hard to say anything" of libidinal dynamics outside the ego, but it is fairly certain that, rather than a reserve or a resource at one's disposal, libidinal energy in those psychic regions *is* what or who the subject itself is. Since, however, we are speculating about a situation before and beyond primary narcissism, what or who this subject is cannot be distinguished from the other—indeed, from a vast number of others, whether human or not—who instigate libidinal flows. Here, as in vegetal life, the one *is* the other. Auto-eroticism, in which "satisfaction is obtained from the subject's own body and extraneous objects are disregarded" (SE 11: 44), is, by the same token, a hetero-eroticism, the eroticism of the other.

Without libidinal ecologies, the purely ego-based libidinal economy is woefully incomplete. Primary narcissism emerges along with the ego itself, and the rest fades by comparison; the ego is the great innovation of libidinal development and the invention of libidinal economy. To a certain extent, the economic model of psychic life and desire will keep eclipsing other possibilities, but in the 1911 notes on a case of paranoia (namely, that of Judge Schreber), Freud makes a crucial observation: "In paranoia the liberated libido becomes attached to the ego, and is used for the aggrandizement of the ego. A return is thus made to the stage of narcissism (known to us from the development of the libido), in which a person's only sexual object is his own ego" (SE 12: 72).

The workings of libidinal economy are akin to the paranoid aggrandizement of the ego, if on a smaller scale. When the ego serves as a reservoir of libidinal cathexes, object choices are always the ego's self-choice, insofar as these cathexes never really detach from the ego. The dynamics of libidinal ecology are the key to breaking out of the tyranny of the ego, which would otherwise be "a person's only sexual object." In libidinal ecology, the ego itself is set free from the role of a reservoir, a resource of libidinal energies cooped up in it, and, at the same time, the only significant point of reference, the auto-affective love object. Instead, the ego becomes a mediator, the essentially relational channel and a purveyor between the reality principle and the pleasure principle, self and other, the human and the other-than-human, who also dwells within ourselves.

M

Melancholy variations

Reflections on mourning and melancholia become more relevant still in the age of environmental devastation than they were more than one hundred years ago, in 1915, when Freud first penned them. Aware of their relevance, psychologist Renée Lertzman pays close attention to "the *lived experience* of environmental degradation," which entails "environmental melancholia," understood as "an arrested, inchoate form of mourning [. . .] at the heart of much of the inaction in response to environmental degradation."[1]

Lertzman is not alone in interpreting melancholia in terms of a merely "arrested," or incomplete, mourning and subsequent paralysis. Schianaia agrees with her verdict, attributing it, at least in part, to the amorphousness of the object that is lost when it comes to a livable environment: "When we deal with the climate issue, it is difficult to individuate the object of the work of mourning and thus more difficult than, for example, mourning the loss of a person."[2] Judith Butler similarly defines melancholia as "a disavowed mourning,"[3] presupposing the conceptual primacy and positivity of mourning, not only as a desirable process to undergo in the case of loss but also as the absolute point of reference, without which melancholia makes no sense. In turn, melancholia is granted a merely derivative identity (perhaps even a non-identity), as the failure, absence, or arrest of mourning, so much so that it is treated as mourning's "inchoate form."

In sharp contrast to contemporary interpretations, Freud does not treat melancholia as an insubstantial shadow of mourning. Melancholia is neither the paralysis nor the suspension nor the disorganization of mourning; it boasts dynamics of its own. It is virtually impossible to tackle environmental melancholia without an appreciation of these dynamics.

Freud begins with an overlap between the two reactions to loss, namely "the same painful frame of mind, the same loss of interest in the external world [...], the same loss of capacity to adopt any new love of object (which would mean replacing him) and the same turning away from any activity that is not connected with thoughts of him" (SE 14: 244). Mourning and melancholia share the state of *inhibition*, responsible for all of these dispositions, moods, and an overall withdrawal from the world and from activity in it. This means that, in environmental crises and concerns, inaction cannot be an exclusive feature of environmental melancholia, since it is part of the shared character of mourning *and* melancholia. Nor is it possible to translate the loss of a beloved object *in* the world—the loss instigating mourning and melancholia alike—into being on the verge of losing the livable world as a whole. More than the "amorphousness" of the lost object, it is this non-translatability of different kinds of losses into each other's terms that ought to preoccupy us.

In the midst of the First World War, when Freud formulates his thoughts on the subject of melancholia, he still does not contemplate the real possibility of total world destruction, even though it must have weighed on his mind at the time. After all, in the same year (1915) Freud jots down his famous "Thoughts for the Times of War and Death," where he speaks of the great disillusionment triggered by war, "the destruction of an illusion" concerning the benefits of advanced civilization, including the mitigation of violence and brutality by upholding high "moral standards" (SE 14: 280). In an analogous way, the environmental crisis potentially destroys the illusion of "nature's" infinite capacity for regeneration, with the proviso that this latter illusion is more deep-seated, because older than "civilization" itself. (Freud notes that "we welcome illusions because they spare us unpleasurable feelings, and enable us to enjoy satisfactions instead" [SE 14: 280]. The illusion of infinite regenerability spares the "unpleasurable feelings" that are connected to death and finitude. This illusion persistently converts death into the dawn of a new life.)

Where the trajectories of mourning and melancholia diverge is with regard to the *experience* and *locus* of loss. "The melancholic displays something else besides which is lacking in mourning," writes Freud, "an extraordinary diminution in his self-regard, an impoverishment of his ego on a grand scale. In mourning, it is the world which has become poor and empty; in melancholia it is the ego itself. The patient represents his ego to us as worthless, incapable of any achievement and morally despicable; he reproaches himself, vilifies himself and expects to be cast out and punished. He abases himself before everyone and commiserates with his own relatives for being connected with someone so unworthy" (SE 14: 246).

We may easily spot in Freud's description of the uniquely melancholic propensity a misanthropic reaction to the environmental disaster: humanity is a parasite on the body of planet Earth, and it would be better for our species to be wiped out; the "world without us" will be an idyllic place of interspecies flourishing; we are worthless and deserve to be extinct. Freud attributes these and related reactions to the emptying out of an ego in the grip of melancholia, but an ego perceived as separate and *ab initio* posited at loggerheads with the world is, in its presumed fullness, already impoverished and emptied out. Not putting *it* in question and keying in solely on the poverty of the world is still being under the spell of melancholia.

It follows that environmental mourning cannot proceed along a transformative track without accounting for melancholia and taking it onboard. If relations to others, including other-than-human living beings and ecosystems, are constitutive of the I, then the massive loss of plant and animal species, not to mention of breathable air and fertile topsoils, is an emptying out of the ego as much as of the world. "Ecology" is not an external object, not an immense and amorphous totality of everything and everyone in existence, but the articulation of the inside and the outside. Before environmental destruction takes place, ecological devastation is palpable in severing the variable, constantly self-reconfiguring relations between these poles. Indeed, the polarization of mourning and melancholia beyond the features they have in common may be due to this prior ecological devastation, resulting in a situation where the impoverishment of the ego (melancholia) and that of the world (mourning) are perceived as diametrically opposed.

The sadomasochism ingrained into the ego–superego dynamic may explain the resigned acceptance of, if not the tacit rejoicing in, the punishment meted out in the shape of the environmental crisis and the possibility of human extinction. The crisis (of any variety) is seen as the externalized embodiment of a harsh superego; the punishing consequences of the crisis are received as self-punishment. In commentaries on the disproportionately large responsibility of the Western, white, wealthy, male portion of humankind for the current state of the world, this sadomasochism is further refined, exacerbated or rejected depending on the identity in question. But assignments of responsibility function at the level of rational calculations and autonomous subjectivity, not reaching the deeper layers of unconscious motivations that are often self-subverting. Below that level, primary masochism is a form of the death instinct, unleashed against the self and the other there where the other is and is not the self, where the world is and is not the ego. Hence, de-cathecting from that other is always de-cathecting from oneself.

Having acknowledged the autochthonous workings of melancholia, Freud affirms that it may disclose something not just about the melancholic but about the human condition more generally speaking. The melancholic "must surely be right in some way and be describing something that is as it seems to him to be [...] He also seems to us justified in certain other self-accusations; it is merely that he has a keener eye for the truth than other people who are not melancholic [...] We only wonder why a man has to be ill before he can be accessible to a truth of this kind" (SE 14: 246). Like subsequent generations of psychologists, Freud realizes that melancholics (or depressed people in contemporary parlance) are more realistic about the world and about themselves than people who do not suffer from this affliction.[4] This is a crucial point: ecology incites widespread interest precisely when it is badly compromised and nearing a global collapse. It is more readily accessible under the sign of felt negativity, illness, suffering, disordering, maladjustment; ecological thought comes with a hefty price tag. We are accessible to ourselves in a like manner. Truth value is the surplus-value of melancholia.

Another Freudian observation concerning melancholia has a special bearing on the psychology of contemporary world-loss. Although a harsh superego is given free rein in denigrating the subject as the culprit behind the catastrophe, unworthy of existence, it proceeds in the absence of an important affective ingredient: "Feelings of shame in front of other people . . . are lacking in the melancholic, or at least they are not prominent in him. One might emphasize the presence in him of an almost opposite trait of insistent communicativeness which finds satisfaction in self-exposure" (SE 14: 247).

While (predominantly in the West) the melancholy response to ecological devastation entails the outpouring of self-denigration, it creates value out of the exaggerated attention to one's own valuelessness, to one's worthlessness as an individual or as a representative of a given group. Self-denigration, in effect, becomes a virtue, to be paraded for all to see in an extreme case of *virtue signaling*. "Satisfaction in self-exposure" is the unconscious positivity within the bleak negativity of melancholy.

Freud further hypothesizes that the emptying out of the ego in melancholy self-beratement is a substitute for violent accusations originally intended for the loved one ("we perceive that the self-reproaches are reproaches against a loved object which have been shifted away from it to the patient's own ego" [SE 14: 248]). Faced with "the end of the world" in the apocalyptic script of a global ecological collapse or a thermonuclear world war, the question is what arouses a melancholy reaction: the loss of the world *as such* or of myself *in* it (where "myself" is not limited to the immediate body and the mind I claim as my own, but, rather, encompasses my imagined posthumous futures, be their carriers the children or the works, the significant relations or the overall legacy, I leave behind)? The beloved object, which is shifted onto the ego of the melancholic, is likewise ambiguous. It may range from past certainties about survival and regeneration now proven untenable to unsustainable lifestyles or, again, the world itself. Since the melancholic subject's identification with that hyper-valorized object was remarkably strong, its loss is taken to be a loss of self.

And that is where the most memorable lines of Freud's essay appear. As a result of "an *identification* of the ego with the abandoned object," "the shadow of the object fell upon the ego [. . .] In this way, an object-loss was transformed into an ego-loss and the conflict between the ego and the loved person into a cleavage between the critical activity of the ego and the ego as altered by identification" (SE 14: 249). The best cinematic rendition of this dramatic situation is Lars von Trier's 2011 *Melancholia*, where a rogue planet (called, precisely, Melancholia) is on a collision course with planet Earth. As the other planet approaches, its shadow literally falls on the terrestrial landscape, eclipses the Sun and stamps the sky and the earth alike with the encroaching death. It bears repeating that when object loss refers to the immense non-object that is a livable environment or the world, the melancholic position of identification with the lost object becomes objectively justifiable. But even if that object is more circumscribed than that, melancholy still fulfills its truth function within the framework of a relational ontology, in which the ego does not survive the loss of all or most of its cathexes to others. In the footsteps of Otto Rank, Freud nonetheless attributes wholesale identification, casting a permanent shadow of object loss on the ego, to narcissism and to the regressive dynamics it betokens (SE 14: 249–50).

The creativity of melancholia, if we are to believe Freud, lies in a narcissistic inflation of the ego masquerading as its absolute deflation. In our terms, berating humanity as a parasite on the planetary body—the parasite worthy of extermination—is tantamount to a species narcissism, secretly taking pride in having achieved planet-scale effects in the age of the Anthropocene. Ecologically inflected misanthropy is, in a speculative reversal reminiscent of Hegel's dialectics, the height of anthropocentrism. The critique of human privilege and of species bias (from deep ecology onwards) is the undoing of the knots of cathexis, the liberation of libidinal energy still bound to the lost object, who is the human at the evolutionary or theological apex, casting the longest shadow on the ego and motivating an interminable narcissistic melancholy.

Much in Freud's text speaks in favor of the above interpretation of cutting-edge responses to the environmental crisis. An actual death need not be the trigger of melancholia, which may be provoked in "situations of being slighted, neglected or disappointed" (SE 14: 251). At the vanguard of young people, school-aged climate activists feel slighted, neglected and disappointed by not being given a chance to have a future propitious to a healthy, satisfactory life, nor by having a say in decisions made in the present that will have huge impact on that future. *In extremis*, these feelings may propel "the tendency to suicide" (SE 14: 252), which would be an individual reflection of (or protest against) the collective suicide of the human species. David Buckel's self-immolation in New York's Prospect Park in 2019, protesting the rapid environmental destruction of the planet, is a case in point here.

Still, the melancholic condition goes further than that; it bespeaks an unconscious relation to finitude, to a death from which the ego is not exempt, despite all its everyday illusions: "The analysis of melancholia now shows that the ego can kill itself only if, owing to the return of the object-cathexis, it can treat itself as an object—if it is able to direct against itself the hostility which relates to an object and which represents the ego's original reaction to objects in the external world" (SE 14: 252). It is the closest the unconscious itself comes to the experience of time and death, exactly when the egoic interface between it and the outside world is irreparably damaged. In a ménage à trois with Hegel and Freud, we may refer to this as "the unconscious self-consciousness," which, devoid of the mechanisms of symbolization, can only find fulfillment in the act of killing oneself.

Not only does Freud discard the currently popular notion of melancholia as a deficient form of mourning, but he also bestows on melancholia the title of a complex—that is, a broader template of libidinal organization (or disorganization) as with the Oedipus complex. "The complex of melancholia," he suggests, "behaves like an open wound, drawing to itself cathectic energies [...] from all directions, and emptying the ego until it is totally impoverished" (SE 14: 253). Other complexes mobilize libidinal energies in patterns of cathexes that are relatively stable and reproducible. Occasionally, an issue (a Cause) may emerge which is so galvanizing that it draws all mental and political energies to itself. Melancholia undoes such a buildup characteristic of other complexes; it gathers cathexes only to squander them, harnessing Eros itself to the work of Thanatos. It is, therefore, a complex of de-complexification and of de-cathexis.

Ecological thought and environmental activism participate in the twenty-first-century melancholia complex, fixated on destruction, devastation, doom, rebellion (as in Extinction Rebellion), and intense opposition devoid of a *position*. These elements of negativity cannot be simply shrugged off; it is necessary to work through them, rather than to act them out. And our task is to come up with a post-negative appreciation of ecology, as well as with philosophies of nature that do not succumb to the melancholia temptation of our age.

N

Negative ecology

Ecological discourses and practices burst on the historical scene and thrive under the sign of negativity. It is when the planetary dwelling is in the state of disarray and on the verge of crumbling that the act of dwelling becomes theoretically visible and thematizable. Dwelling is habitual and unconscious—the hotspot of what indicates psychical inertia. What are the implications of bringing it (never completely, to be sure) to consciousness through the abruptness and shock of a crisis, subsequently articulated in words and pondered conduct?

The prismatic interplay of negations in psychoanalysis may shed light on the various senses of "negative ecology."

First, negation leads back to the absolute positivity of the unconscious, and it ends there where the unconscious begins. In a footnote, which he added to the discussion of the "Dora case" in 1923, Freud announces: "There is another very remarkable and entirely trustworthy form of confirmation from the unconscious, which I had not recognized at the time when this was written: namely, an exclamation on the part of the patient of 'I didn't think that', or 'I didn't think of that'. This can be translated point-blank into: 'Yes, I was unconscious of that'" (SE 7: 57). Not-thinking *is* thinking without realizing it: the "no" becomes a "yes" under the Midas touch of the unconscious. Before the rise of ecology as a movement and a theoretico-practical attitude, we didn't think of dwelling, which means that, yes, we were unconscious of that. *That* includes being in place, feeling at home there, feeling at ease in one's own body and its interactions with the environment. To dwell, to exist, one must be to a large extent unconscious of all *that*, whereas pain, hunger, a lack of shelter, persecution, disability, a constant sense of danger, and similar factors disrupt these unconscious routines.

The unconscious, then, endeavors to transform every *no* into a *yes*, but, in order to do so, it must register the *no*, heeding its negativity, which is a difficult task since "there is no such thing at all as an unconscious 'No'" (SE 7: 57). The apparatus of consciousness, in its negotiation between the reality principle and the pleasure principle that does not tolerate frustration, must establish communication and translation mechanisms between affirmation and negation, including sundry stratagems and defenses that, often at a high psychological cost, flip the *no* into a *yes*. Much of denial and, indeed, denialism as such are driven by these mechanisms: assertions that there is no anthropogenic ecosystems' collapse, no mass extinction, or no catastrophic climate change imply an unconscious *yes* to the unchanging routines of the unconscious (our psychic dwelling) even when the biological-environmental dwelling is severely threatened and undermined.

For Freud, the more vociferous the *no*, the stronger the force of repression that converts the unconscious *yes* into its opposite: "The 'No' uttered by a patient after a repressed thought has been presented to his conscious perception for the first time does no more than register the existence of a repression and its severity; it acts, as it were, as a gauge of the repression's strength" (SE 7: 58). In debates concerning catastrophic climate change, there are always at least three sides: those who acknowledge it, those who deny it, and the forces of repression that balance on the unstable edge of the *yes-no*. Nor is the outright acknowledgment of the depth of the problem so straightforward as it seems: uttering "yes" (and sometimes "yes!") with regard to mass extinction and human extinction, the rising sea levels and global temperatures, deforestation and desertification may be indicative of unconsciously *wanting* that these happen, retroactively transforming fate into one's desire or desiring one's fate in a sentiment Nietzsche acclaimed as *amor fati*. When "'No' signifies the desired 'Yes'" (SE 7: 59), the negation is twice removed from the subject's desire, which is at a single remove from the affirmation, unconsciously embracing that which is affirmed, however terrible it might be.

Probably the most famous treatment of the "no" and its relation (or non-relation) to the unconscious may be found in Freud's 1925 essay,

"Negation." There, the initial association is treated as psychologically more important than its subsequent rejection: if the analysand says, "You ask who this person in the dream can be. This is *not* my mother," then the analysts' interpretation is "So it *is* his mother." "In our interpretation," Freud explains, "we take the liberty of disregarding the negation and of picking out the subject-matter alone of the association" (SE 19: 235). It would not be far-fetched to extend this line of argumentation to climate change denial: "This is *not* climate change (but just an isolated instance of extreme weather" means that the denier is unconsciously confirming, "So it *is* climate change." As with the logic of the dream, the issue has to do with something that is not empirically accessible, that is deduced from long-term trends, changes of patterns, and probabilities of certain events occurring in the absence of anthropogenic climate effects. And, since the confrontations of climate change deniers and those who affirm its reality do not resemble a coldly dispassionate discussion, the psychoanalytic strategy of mistrusting the negation might be effective.

To mistrust the *no* is not to dismiss it, nor—with and as it—the position of the deniers. It is, rather, to commence the analytic work, in the course of which "we can see how in this [negation, MM] the intellectual function is separated from the affective process" (SE 19: 236). The *not happening* added to climate change is intellectual self-censorship, thanks to which repressed material (here: the realization that this *is* climate change) is permitted to surface and to be articulated at the level of consciousness. The addition is "the function of intellectual judgment" (SE 19: 236), which does not cancel out affects, simmering beneath it. The anxieties, worries, and fears are not quelled by the *no*; if anything, they grow more oppressive and assume other twisted forms in concerns with individual safety, a tenuous self-isolation from foreign elements, and a whole range of other, typically right-wing affects.

For Freud, intellectualization results from the sublimation of "raw" libidinal energy, which he traces back to the oral stage at the roots of negation. "Expressed in the language of the oldest—the oral—instinctual impulses, the judgment is: 'I should like to eat this' or 'I should like to spit it out'; and, put more generally: 'I should like to take this into myself and to keep that out'" (SE 19: 237). Affirmation keeps what it affirms inside the subject; negation strives to maintain the negated outside. But how would it be possible to "spit out" climate change if the climate is *what holds us in it*, enveloping us, swallowing us up (or spitting us out when it is not propitious to life), and so acting as an impersonal subject in relation to us? Conversely, what would taking the climate (climate change, climate collapse . . .) into oneself look like for those do affirm it? What would climate justice look and feel like then?

As far as I can tell, there are two possible approaches to "eating" climate change and environmental devastation. On the one hand, *identification*, coming to desire extinction (at least of the human species) and celebrating the ensuing vision of the "world without us"; on the other, *slow digestion*, mourning, and a gradual transformation of the affective relation to and the intellectual construal of ecology, neither idealizing nor disavowing it. Resetting the dynamics of introjection and ejection, of incorporation and excretion, such psychical metabolism is the bloodline of meaningful environmental action, as is the next step Freud insists upon, namely, the development of the "reality-ego" from the "initial pleasure-ego."

With the development of this other ego from the one driven exclusively by pleasure, "it is [. . .] no longer a question of whether what has been perceived (a thing) shall be taken into the ego or not, but of whether something which is in the ego as a presentation can be rediscovered in perception (reality) as well" (SE 19: 237). The reality-ego is capable of tolerating *dis*pleasure—hence, negativity—rather than immediately rejecting or ejecting it in the manner of the pleasure-ego—to the extent that this negativity is acknowledged as existing in reality. Nevertheless, the function of reality-testing with respect to anthropogenic climate change has to be delegated to science and its technological apparatus singularly equipped to register and track such grand-scale processes. Due to a gap that opens between the individual reality-ego, which deals with what is perceived, and its techno-scientific supplement, conspiracy theories proliferate. In the last instance, though, denialism is symptomatic of the unconscious unwillingness to take the extra step Freud describes, to come to terms with negativity and to keep even what is disagreeable because it agrees with external reality.

Lest one be under the impression that the development of the reality-ego represents "progress," Freud points out that reality testing is conservative in its character. Because thinking has the function of recollection, or re-presentation of what has been perceived in the past, "the first and the immediate aim [...] of reality-testing is not to *find* an object in real perception which corresponds to the one presented, but to *refind* such an object, to convince oneself that it is still there" (SE 19: 237–8). The gaze of the observer assessing the present with the view to the future is fundamentally backward-looking: *voilà* yet another legacy of ancient thought that is alive in Freud's psychoanalysis. But, in the case of climate change and the environmental crisis, what is one meant to "refind" in reality-testing? Could it be the perceived experience of negativity (of hunger, for example), which threatens survival?

Learning from a crisis would require learning how to deal with negativity without unconsciously transforming it into an aspect of positivity, as in hallucinating about food, being convinced that one can produce it out of oneself (sucking one's finger), or that the source of nourishment is under one's complete control and can be called upon, materializing at will. More concretely, one would refind the negativity of frustrated physiological needs, inseparable from unconscious desire, in the absence of breathable air or drinkable water, against the backdrop of the degradation of fertile topsoils, frequent storms and floods or droughts, and unbearable temperatures. These objects or non-objects cannot be recovered individually, which is why, corresponding to collective reality-testing by techno-science, it is necessary to resort to a joint subjectivity, tasked with acting in a non-hallucinatory, non-delusional way. Just as "it is evident that a precondition for the setting up of reality-testing is that objects shall have been lost which once brought real satisfaction" (SE 19: 238), so it is obvious that a precondition for the emergence of collective subjectivity is that the individual subject shall have been lost, who once could ensure and experience that satisfaction.

Toward the end of his essay on negation, Freud distributes the affirmative and the negative judgments between "two groups of instincts": "Affirmation—as a substitute for uniting—belongs to Eros; negation—the successor to expulsion—belongs to the instinct of destruction" (SE 19: 239). Although formally this conclusion makes sense, Freud immediately contradicts himself, precisely at the moment of rejoicing in the confirmation of this theoretical insight in clinical experience: "This view of negation fits in very well with the fact that in analysis we never discover a 'no' in the unconscious" (SE 19: 239).

But, if all *no*s are traces of conscious judgment, if, in other words, the unconscious knows no negation, then where do the "instinct of destruction" and the death drive reside?

It could well be that Freud is thinking only of the analytic situation ("the fact that in analysis we never discover . . ."), but then analysis does not go deep enough into the unconscious. Given that, throughout his writings, Freud contends that the unconscious knows no negation and, by implication, no death,[1] the death drive, as a striving to dissolve the tensions inherent to life and to return to the undisturbed quietude of inorganic existence, might be an amplification of the temporary dissolution of tensions in the satisfaction achieved on the basis of the pleasure principle. It follows that destruction is not the motivation but, on the contrary, a consequence of this radical striving "beyond" the pleasure principle, which intensifies something of this very principle. As for "negative ecology," the *no* it revolves around is destructive only in a derivative sense, taking note of and endeavoring to transform from within the destruction that is structuring "external" reality.

In a late paper (dated "1937"), "Constructions in Analysis," Freud revisits the issue of the *yes* and the *no* uttered by the analysand and the credence or non-credence the analyst gives to these judgments. In essence, Freud sees analysis itself *as* construction: the task of the analyst is "to make out what has been forgotten from the traces which it has left behind or, more correctly, to *construct* it" (SE 23: 259). The construction does not mean that, thanks to the equivalent of detective work, the analyst will arrive at the original forgotten or repressed experience, but it does allude to the job of "refinding" an object in the course of reality-testing—a psychical function, which the analyst temporarily assumes on behalf of the analysand. The materials of this construction are notable for their relation to affirmation and negation: they are the *yes*es of a *no*, the positive (if twisted) traces of an absence, of the forgotten, the repressed appearing and disappearing under erasure. And isn't now, in the twenty-first century, ecology itself, comprehended as a shared planetary dwelling, that *no*, which is accessible solely through its fragmentary remnants?

Freud leads us to the above insight, or at least a hypothesis, via an example he gives: the analyst's "work of construction, or, if it is preferred, of reconstruction, resembles to a great extent an archaeologist's excavation of some dwelling-place that has been destroyed and buried or of some ancient edifice" (SE 23: 259). He goes on to list other formal parallels between the two occupations, including difficulties in dating ancient artifacts or many missing materials that need to be inferred for the reconstruction to work. The crux of the matter, though, is that the aspiration of psychoanalysis is to reconstruct psychic habitability, buried under piles of ruins. Similarly, negative ecology, in the constructive or reconstructive sense, takes the form of a psychoanalytic archeology on a planetary scale. Whatever the materials utilized in the two endeavors, they boil down to the *yes* and the *no*, each of the judgments rendered non-transparent by its complicity with, and even the masking of, the other.

O

Obsessive self-blame

In the process of reckoning with historical injustices, discrimination, exploitation, and worse, we witness a polarized response to such legacies. On the one hand, descendants of the privileged (white, European, male, heteronormative in various combinations or taken separately) may deny any and all responsibility and culpability—a denial, which, given all the available evidence, cannot but take the form of repression. On the other hand, representatives of the same class, gender, racial, sexual, and other identity categories may experience intense, and often disproportionate, feelings of guilt.[1] Blame for the past misdeeds of others, not least of which is environmental pollution and devastation, is taken upon oneself, often with excessive zeal, accompanied by practices of self-punishment that range from verbal self-depreciation to ascetic, ritually exculpatory behaviors. Among these reactions, obsessive neuroses prevail and culminate in dis-identification, or a refusal to identify any longer with the group to which one belongs (which is another strategy of shirking responsibility altogether, effectively repeating the gesture of denial, albeit without holding onto the dominant identity).

Freud's most extensive treatment of obsessional ideation and behavior may be found in the case histories of "Little Hans" and the "Rat Man." The affective basis of obsessions may be fears or wishes, though, as Freud has it, "obsessional structures can correspond to every sort of psychical act. They can be classed as wishes, temptations, impulses, reflections, doubts, commands, or prohibitions" (SE 10: 221–2). The universality of obsessive psychic forms puts them, within what Freud himself terms "the phenomenology of obsessional thinking" (SE 10: 222), on a par with phenomenological intentionality, which is proper to every psychic act of directing-oneself-toward ... The key to obsession, however, is that it obstructs the modulation of the psychic regard: it is the same wish, temptation, impulse, and so on that stands out in the center of one's psychic existence, gradually muscling out or at least occluding all other wishes, impulses, and temptations. Where obsessions differ from simple fixations, or the "stuckness" of the drive, is in their relation to guilt. Freud again: "In the year 1896 I defined obsessional ideas as 'transformed self-reproaches which have re-emerged from repression and which always relate to some sexual act that was performed with pleasure in childhood'" (SE 10: 221).

It becomes a little clearer why obsessive self-blaming is so prevalent in the age of climate collapse: it builds upon the psychic architecture of obsession, which already includes self-reproach, magnifying this sentiment manifold. Freud is also unambiguous on the motivations of obsessive ideation, namely the guilt experienced as a result of "some sexual act that was performed with pleasure in childhood." A classical Freudian approach would then attribute the obsession with one's involvement in historical injustices or in the destruction of the environment to a displacement and distortion (still under the influence of repression) of the original sexually charged act (SE 10: 225).

What if, nonetheless, the guilty pleasure in question has to do with the privilege one (and/or one's ancestors) enjoyed at the expense of other, oppressed human groups or of the other-than-human world? Indeed, the positive pleasure derived from enjoying undue privilege might be mixed with the sadistic pleasure drawn from the suffering and destitution of those, at whose expense it is derived. The sexual and sexualized roots of these pleasures are also rather self-evident.

The reason for examining the unconscious affective background of ecological thought and activism, throughout this study in general and in the case of obsessional ideation and behavior in particular, is to ask what they are all about, beneath or behind their overtly stated motivations. Concerns for the environment? For future generations? One's own wounded narcissism, illusion of mastery and control? An environment propitious to human existence and future generations *as* the extensions of the narcissistic sphere? These are not idle questions, because, when left unanswered, unconscious or semi-conscious displacements and obsessional projections onto ecology weaken the stated objectives of eco-activism and eco-philosophy. That is why psychoanalysis (or, more broadly, self-analysis) is needed, in a sustained and "interminable" mode, for any viable ecological program.

In the 1894 paper, "Obsessions and Phobias," Freud discerns two components in every obsession: "(1) an idea that forces itself upon the patient; (2) an associated emotional state" (SE 3: 74). The obsessional idea substitutes for another one: "the original (incompatible) idea has been replaced by another idea, the substituted idea" (SE 3: 77). Acting upon this substitute idea is meant to be a protection and a relief measure with respect to the subterranean impact of the original idea, memory, and the like. Here, obsessive self-flagellation seems to be inconsistent with Freud's theory, unless we put forward the hypothesis that attacking oneself this way serves to prevent (or to eclipse) another, still more intolerable and deeper sense of guilt. Could it be that *ecological* self-blame, which is also used as a tool underwriting the culpability of others, levels down all the geographical and geopolitical, class, gender, and sexual differences? If so, then the homogenous mass of demonized "parasitic humanity" and of the idealized "future generations" covers over and attempts to dissipate those differences, along with the tensions they presuppose.

Two years later, in another paper, Freud will recognize the fundamental role of self-blame in obsessions that are "nothing other than *reproaches addressed by the subject to himself on account of* [. . .] *anticipated sexual enjoyment*, but reproaches distorted by an unconscious psychical work of transformation and substitution" (SE 3: 155). In the case of obsessive ecological self-blame, the reproach as such is obvious; what is distorted is its underlying cause. Moreover, once we substitute for sexual enjoyment other sorts of enjoyment related to one's everyday life (driving a car that runs on diesel or other combustible sources of energy, consuming products that have a disproportionately polluting effect on the environment, and so forth), excessive reproach comes to counterbalance the benefits derived from these. Of course, one can do one's best to "minimize one's carbon footprint," excluding as much as possible polluting practices and materials from one's daily routine, but new concerns will intrude instead: for instance, if I drive an electric car, then I might be worried about the lithium battery it uses on account of the mining its production entails and the problems of disposal at the end of the battery's lifetime. Tellingly, psychic and material substitutions have much in common and, in this particular case, reinforce one another without breaking the spiral of obsessive self-reproach.

Freud pursues the association of obsessional ideation, affect, and action with self-blame in "Further Remarks on the Neuro-Psychoses of Defense" (1896). This is the very paper he cites in his well-known case histories of "Little Hans" and the "Rat Man." And the sexual etiology of obsession (with the associated sense of guilt emerging from the partial lifting of repression), for which Freudian psychoanalysis is frequently criticized, cannot be taken lightly in this context, as much as in the context of the ecological blame game.

The two moments of substitution, yielding obsessive self-reproach, which Freud pinpoints are as follows: "first, something contemporary is put in the place of something past; and secondly, something sexual is replaced by something analogous to it that is not sexual" (SE 3: 170). Attaining an existential pitch, ecological concern is surely "something contemporary" that replaces repressed material from the past, and it is not sexual, as opposed to what it replaces. But it cannot free itself from repression and the sphere of sexuality, given that "*whenever a neurotic obsession emerges in the psychical sphere, it comes from repression*" (SE 3: 171). Whether it has to do with a greater degree of repression of sexuality among young people today or whether we are dealing with the transfer of libidinal relations onto the other-than-human world, a neurotic eco-obsession cannot be unfastened from a sexualized ontology.

So, why are obsessions with ecology and the guilt they are loaded with feckless at best and counterproductive at worst? Because, although they dictate many nitty-gritty details of a subject's existence, they are recognized by this very subject as alien and untrue, not really deserving to be believed: "The fact that the obsessional ideas and everything derived from them meet with no belief [from the subject] is no doubt because at their first repression the defensive symptom of *conscientiousness* has been formed and that that symptom, too, acquires an obsessional force. The subject's certainty of having lived a moral life throughout the whole period of his successful defense makes it impossible for him to believe the self-reproach which his obsessional idea involves" (SE 3: 174). In other words, an effective obsession that fulfills its protective function undermines its own logic: self-reproach coincides with extreme self-righteousness. As a defense mechanism, obsessional self-blaming by climate, vegan, and a plethora of other activists may go hand-in-hand with a lack of availability to outside critique and a sense of moral superiority over those who do not belong to the in-group. It is a sign that the defense mechanism of obsessive neurosis has worked: the belief in "having lived a moral life throughout the whole period" of obsessive ideation and action undermines the grounds of obsessive self-blame, which is experienced in the absence of belief in its validity.

The structural similarities between obsessive-compulsive behavior and religion (or at least a "caricature of religion" [SE 13: 73]) did not escape Freud's attention. In *The Future of an Illusion*, Freud concludes that "religion would thus be the universal obsessional neurosis of humanity; like the obsessional neurosis of children, it arose out of the Oedipus complex, out of the relation to the father." And he continues: "Our analogy does not, to be sure, exhaust the essential nature of religion. If, on the one hand, religion brings with it obsessional restrictions, exactly as an individual obsessional neurosis does, on the other hand it comprises a system of wishful illusions together with the disavowal of reality" (SE 21: 43). We might add, in keeping with Freud's line of thought, that such a religion would be shorn of belief thanks to the effectiveness of its belief.

Allowing ecology to enjoy the status of a new religion is dangerous because ritualistic "obsessional restrictions" may then have to do more with individual and collective neuroses than with effective plans to combat global heating, biodiversity loss, or the degradation of topsoils. The compensations for these restrictions are the "wishful illusions" of salvation *if only* no animal meat is consumed, no fossil fuels are burnt, all plastic is recycled (fill in the blanks) . . . The danger is that the course of ecological action would be, in these cases, predicated on disavowal, the simultaneous acknowledgment and repudiation of ecological complexity and of the equally multiple sources of ecological disasters, let alone our own motivations to act and to think "ecologically." It would then be no more than a symptom of obsessive-compulsive behavior, of a neurotic acting-out.

The above does not by any means imply that the thinking of ecology should be prioritized to the detriment of ecological action; rather, the latter should find its banisters in thought oriented as much outwardly as inwardly, in a self-analysis that persists with and adumbrates this action. To return to the two case studies with which we started, an overemphasis placed on thinking signals, rather than critical maturity, an obsession-dominated regression. Here "preparatory acts become substituted for the final decision, thinking replaces acting, and, instead of the substitutive act, some thought preliminary to it asserts itself with all the force of compulsion" (SE 10: 244). Regression from acting to thinking is an obsession, which is drawn to endless navel-gazing, self-blame, irresolvable doubt. But because action is inevitable, it is decoupled from thinking understood in terms of its preparatory framework and, along with obsessive ideation, assumes the form of a compulsion. Chronic doubt presents itself as ironclad self-certainty, while self-blame recedes from view behind the facade of self-righteousness.

P

Plants and psychoanalysis

Freud says precious little about plants in his writings, but the few mentions of them which we find in his oeuvre are noteworthy. The most extensive treatment of plants in Freud's texts is related to his own "dream of the botanical monograph." The report of the dream is very short, followed by a long chain of free associations. These require additional analysis, seeking the lacunae in Freud's self-understanding, the sites of repression that are not coincidentally vegetal. But, first things first, here is the account of the dream: "*I had written a monograph on a certain plant. The book lay before me and I was at the moment turning over a folded colored plate. Bound up in each copy there was dried specimen of the plant, as though it had been taken from an herbarium*" (SE 4: 167).

Before anything else, it is important to note that Freud textualizes plants. He is taken not by the plants themselves, which are not even minimally individuated by means of naming their species, but by their botanical study and the resultant monograph. The only trace of vegetal matter in the dream is a "dried specimen of the plant, as though it had been taken from an herbarium." Everything in the dream is dry: a scientific study, a dried specimen, the herbarium analogy. But who if not a master of psychoanalysis would be capable of discovering the juiciest and most piquant details in the midst of such dryness?

The epistemophilic drive, the desire to know, is itself a mutation of the sexual instinct, rooted in the early researches of children into their origins and, hence, into where babies come from, giving rise to infantile theories of sexuality and birth. That *plants* are at the core of scientific knowing, rather than merely being there and flourishing, in the midst of Freud's dream is symptomatic of unease with allowing them to express more fully the blossoming of sexuality, or, rather than unease, the disavowal of the plants–sexuality nexus. In effect, Freud offers his dream as an example of "indifferent materials" and "indifferent experiences," which, in dream-work, "take the place of psychically significant ones" (SE 4: 176). But the extent to which plants and their psychical framing are "indifferent material" is doubtful: while traditionally associated with an insensitive and indifferent mode of existence, they are the mainstay of Victorian, highly codified, substitutes for the overt invocations of sexuality. It cannot be the case that this cultural-historic deployment of plants has simply escaped Freud, or, if it did, the slippage itself is exceptionally significant.

Freud's free association extends his plant dream in a dream-like fashion, leading him and the readers from one thought to another, as though he (and we) were pollinators fluttering among flowers. From a memory of seeing a book on cyclamens in the window of a bookstore, he moves to the realization that these are his wife's favorite flowers and to immediate self-reproach "for so rarely remembering to *bring her flowers*" (SE 4: 169). The sexual connotations of "bringing flowers" are too glaring to comment, and Freud quickly passes on to the case of an analysand forgetting to offer flowers to his wife on her birthday, thereby breaking an annual tradition and triggering the wife's deep sadness (SE 4: 170).

Beyond and behind the Victorian "language of flowers" that subtends these associations, there is the fundamental vegetality of psychoanalysis, upon which I have already commented and which has remained opaque to Freud himself. The conceptual link here is Aristotle, with his postulation that the vegetal psychic faculty, *to threptikon*, is the most basic kind of soul, shared by all living beings. Although, within *to threptikon*, Aristotle prioritizes the capacities for nourishment over reproduction and Freud treats ingestion as derivative from sexual ontology, these belong to the principle of vitality initially developed in plants and carried over to other forms of life, including the human. The very co-belonging of nourishment and reproduction, in whatever configuration they may be arranged, is crucial. Freud may not have recognized the significance of plants and, above all, of the vital capacities they embody, but their appearance in his work is symptomatic of more than this or that repressed desire or unfulfilled wish: it evokes the vegetal origins of the pleasure principle, just as the inorganic world stands for the inanimate substratum of the death drive, whither this drive strives to return.

Semantically gliding, superficial, dreamy associations, with which Freud unravels the meanings of the dream about the botanical manuscript, are themselves faithful to the essential superficiality of vegetal life. A deep study of plants, while flashing in the image of the manuscript, is backgrounded by the dynamic form of associative connections. Freud recalls that he "really *had* written something in the nature of a *monograph on a plant*, namely a dissertation on the *coca-plant*, which had drawn Karl Koller's attention to the anesthetic properties of cocaine" (SE 4: 170). So, Freud studied the de-sensitizing (anesthetic) effects of a certain plant (coca), coinciding with the view of the flora as such as insensitive and non-sentient. However, to have an effect on the central nervous system, be it as a stimulant or a painkiller, plants must have had a prior interaction, honed in the course of co-evolution, with the neurotransmitters (such as serotonin or dopamine) they block or stimulate. Unconsciously, the focus on the desensitizing properties of a plant is an acknowledgment of plant sensitivity.

The episode of cocaine study climaxes with a chance association that circles back to the issue of blossoms, blooms, and the overlaps between vegetal sexuality and human sexuality. While discussing with colleagues the events and academic conversations centered on the discovery of cocaine's anesthetic potential, Freud notes that "Professor *Gärtner* (Gardener) and his wife had joined us; and I could not help congratulating them both on their *blooming* looks" (SE 4: 171). Earlier he related "bringing flowers" to the attention one paid to a wife—both his own and the wife of a patient, distressed that her husband had not brought flowers on her birthday. Here, too, it is a professor, whose last name alludes to a vegetal environment and to care for it, and his wife who are said to have "*blooming* looks," in an extension of a compliment to both sexes and an expression of bisexual interest (which elsewhere Freud considers to be the "default" condition of human sexuality). In psychic life guided by constellations of cathexis and libidinal flows, by phantasy that neither knows nor wants to know about formal, conceptual or definitional, institutional, legal, and other sorts of restrictions, these various couples are interchangeable and reversible, both as couples and with respect to their individual parties. If the language of plants, of blooming, bringing flowers, etc. mediates such boundless promiscuity, that is because the pattern of what is so mediated is unconsciously modeled on vegetal sexuality.

The reversibility of sexual relations, where Freud can assume the role of the recipient of flowers from his wife, is evident in the continuing process of his free association. "It occurred to me," he writes, "that artichokes were Compositae, and indeed I might fairly have called them my *favorite flowers*. Being more generous than I am, my wife often brought me back these favorite flowers of mine from the market" (SE 4: 172). Freud confesses that he gets his favorite flowers from his wife more often than she does from him, hinting at a certain sexual dynamic, which masks as "generosity" in his self-analysis. Moreover, with artichokes, the nutritive and the sexual aspects of plant being and of vegetal psychic life extending to human existence merge into one, recapitulating the Aristotelian position.

The analysis in question is part of Freud's 1900 "dream book," *The Interpretation of Dreams*, written well before his discovery of the death drive. Still, much in the dream and its discussion speaks to the issue of death, channeled through plant imagery. One, most readily discernable, element in the shadow of the death drive is the emergence of a dry herbarium specimen in the book, which is itself a tomb for and a monument to the sexually rooted epistemophilic drive. The other is the afterlife, or the afterdeath, of an associated herbarium, devoured by small worms. Freud observes that, when he was in secondary school, the "headmaster once called together the boys from the higher forms and handed over the school's herbarium to them to be looked through and cleaned. Some small *worms*—book-worms—had found their way into it" (SE 4: 171). The preservation of plants is threatened by the worms who devour them, reanimating death itself with another kind of eating, tapping into the capacity for nourishment that resides in the vegetal psychic faculty. Along with his peers, Freud is enjoined to save the herbarium, but in the continuation of the reflection, he identifies with the figure of a bookworm, who renders the powers of destruction indistinguishable from those of saving. How so?

Freud reminisces that, as a university student, he "had developed a passion for collecting and owning books." "I had become a *book-worm*," he adds (SE 4:

172). As a passion, this hobby (described as his "favorite," like artichokes and cyclamens) sits close to the libidinal drives, and it involves hoarding or accumulating (an anal feature) but also poring through, analyzing, biting into, devouring (an oral feature). In their vegetality, books, like herbaria, are the material aspects of the realm of knowledge, feeding the humanimal dwellers, users, and owners of libraries and collections. The confluence of preservation and destruction conveys, nonetheless, a sadistic modification of the instinct, perhaps magnifying the anal-retentive tendency—the desire to destroy destruction itself, to stave death off by devouring it and perishable materials all the better, more thoroughly, more efficiently. Retention and expulsion, the opposite movements of the anal phase, similarly fuse together in Freud's near bankruptcy due to an excessive buying of books (SE 4: 173).

A palpable example of this tendency from an earlier period, likewise raised by Freud in his dreamy analysis of the botanical dream, is what he calls "almost the only plastic memory that I retained from that period of my life [the age of five, MM]" (SE 4: 172). The memory involves the young Freud and his still younger sister "blissfully pulling the book to pieces (leaf by leaf, like an *artichoke*, I found myself saying)" (SE 4: 172). The material analysis of the book presages its ideal-ideational analysis in understanding, though now the damaged herbarium mutates into a damaged book, which is like an artichoke, while Freud and his sister are in the symbolic position of worms, munching on the leaves they pull to pieces.

At this point, Freud interrupts his detailed analysis of the dream (do psychic contents supplant the book, herbaria, and artichokes thanks to the operations of psycho-analysis?), in his words, "for reasons with which we are not concerned" (SE 4: 173). In and of itself, this statement speaks volumes: negation, as Freud himself knows, means its opposite: the unconscious sense of what he conveys is that there *is* a cause for concern and that it is, in fact, so concerning that analysis cannot proceed any further. (Taking the analytic thread up again toward the end of his "dream book," Freud hints that the previously unstated association was with his "thoughts about Italy" [SE 4: 283].) The last image before the interruption is, precisely, that of being a bookworm and of the associated "bibliophile propensities," for which it serves as a "screen memory" (SE 4: 173). Is it the thought of death, with which Freud identifies as a worm, and, more specifically, of the life-and-death of plants (herbaria, pages in books, artichokes . . .) that is at issue? Whatever it may be, Freud *does* continue despite vowing not to, if only to "merely indicate the direction in which it [subsequent analysis, MM] lay" (SE 4: 173).

The direction he indicates is reductionist: diverse threads of dream analysis (among which worms and herbaria are, however, nowhere to be found) are traced back to a conversation with colleagues (in particular with one colleague, Dr. Königstein), which happened on a day previous to the dream and provoked it (SE 4: 173–4). Having said that, Freud immediately locates a "a *second* source of the dream" in "another experience of the same day," namely seeing "a book in a shop-window whose title attracted my attention for a moment but whose subject-matter could scarcely be of interest to me" (SE 4: 174). There is, as we know, no single linear determination of dreamwork; dream images are always overdetermined: the assuredly single source of a dream is supplemented by a second source, apparently without contradiction. Furthermore, the multiple roots of a dream that condenses from a hodgepodge of experiences, unfulfilled wishes, and desires follow a vegetal model of dispersed causality. Not only the content of Freud's dream about the botanical manuscript but also its form, as well as the form of its interpretation and of the interpretation of that interpretation, are vegetal.

In a discussion of overdetermination and condensation, down the line in *The Interpretation of Dreams*, Freud will reiterate (in a condensed format, mind you) his botanical dream and its analysis. He will treat both "botanical" and "manuscript" as "nodal points, upon which a great number of the dream-thoughts converged" (SE 4: 283), which means that they are, by the same token, the nodal points for condensation and overdetermination, the concentration and dispersal of unconscious causes and effects. Dream images are akin to botanical figures—the shapes, colors, textures of leaves, flowers, fruit, branches—that condense from the overdetermined mix of the subterranean and aboveground environments, climates, genetics, seasonal variations and abnormalities, among other factors. These plant forms *express* multiple vectors of co-evolution and ecological dynamics, but they do so indirectly, without a clear linear determination of the effects by their causes. It is not by accident that "the nature of the relation between dream-content and dream-thoughts thus becomes visible" (SE 4: 284) in the singular context of a botanical dream, since plants are all about coming to visibility, tending to and extending into the light, while retaining a close, intimate, unbreakable bond to darkness.

I also have in mind the distinction between manifest and latent dream contents, which is key to Freud's approach and which recaptures the way plants span below- and aboveground environments in their own growth. The idea is that "indifferent" materials, such as botanical specimens or books, displace and supplant psychically important impressions (SE 4: 175). The dream is an intermediary between the latent and the manifest and, again, it is remarkable that Freud paints this image of the dream with the help of the vegetal images and associations featured in a dream of his. After all, plants are also these very intermediaries, the communicative channels between the soil and the atmosphere—for water and humidity as much as for energy and life itself. Hence, Freud refers to "the botanical group of ideas" as "intermediate links" "which formed the bridge between the two experiences of that day, the indifferent and the stirring one" (SE 4: 175–6). The links or the intermediaries, in their turn, are not obstructions to clear understanding that may be decodified and so removed from the analytical path. Instead, they lend the depth, texture, and perhaps even being to psychic life, without which this life falls apart, just as the being of plants is to be found in their interminable intermediacy, without which, committed to one environment only, they perish.

Only exceptionally and episodically do plants reappear in Freud's other writings. One such work with passing mentions of plants is the 1913 *Totem and Taboo*. Although Freud does not spell this out, the two main terms in the title are in an antithetical relation to one another: totem unites the clan, organizing its members into the same social body among themselves and with the ancestral spirit, while taboo divides the clean from the unclean, the sacred from the profane, and, more generally, the permitted from the non-permitted with regard to who one can have sexual relations with in order to avoid incest (SE 13: 2). The synthetic and the analytic elements of totem and taboo will later reemerge in the opposition between Eros and Thanatos, the life instinct and the death drive. These moments are interrelated; each of them harbors the other, but they are mutually exclusive, in the best of dialectical traditions.

A totem, Freud asserts, is "as a rule an animal [. . .] and more rarely a plant or a natural phenomenon (such as rain or water), which stands in a peculiar relation to the whole clan. In the first place, the totem is the common ancestor of the clan and at the same time it is their guardian spirit and helper" (SE 13: 2). With plants, the "whole," into which a clan is to be welded, becomes more nebulous than with the organismic totality of animals: plants are wholes in parts and parts in wholes, rendering the task of unification all but impossible. The distinctions between life and death (hence, Eros and Thanatos) are also exceptionally difficult to make in plants, which is why Freud will exclude them from the "original" group of totem animals, protected by the prohibition of killing (SE 13: 107). That said, the deep affinities of life and death instincts to do with the temporary or permanent satisfaction of desire, respectively, reveal their non-contradictory, vegetal nature, also reflected in the coincidence of retention and expulsion, of the care for and destruction of a herbarium in Freud's train of free associations.

Curiously, the same ambiguity befalls plant taboos, at least in the way Freud describes them (via Wilhelm Wundt). In addition to the taboos related to animals and humans, there is the category of "other objects," which includes plants. "The third class of taboos, which are imposed on trees, plants, houses, and localities, are less stable," Freud writes. "They appear to follow a rule that anything that is uncanny or provokes dread for any reason becomes subject to taboo" (SE 13: 23). Classed together with dwellings (houses, localities), plants are deemed uncanny (*unheimlich*). Their apparent physical stability is consistent with their instability as a "class of taboos"—that is to say, a psychological instability. The plasticity of vegetal sexuality may undermine the strict dividing lines that a taboo draws, especially with regard to incestual relations.

Putting to one side the dubious anthropological method Freud resorts to, it is possible to piece these scant references to plants together in order to draw a psychoanalytic lesson. What they show is that, in plants, synthesis and analysis in mental life are virtually indistinguishable from one another: the death drive blends with the life instinct. The unconscious of plants—which extends beyond their own growing-extending bodies to the transition zones of the soil and the atmosphere, to soil legacy and microclimates influenced by plant ecosystems, such as the rainforest—operates with a seamless unity of the striving to return to inorganic existence (the death drive) and the social, associative gathering of disparate cells, elements, biological kingdoms (the erotic/life instinct). This conclusion is entirely in accord with Freud's analysis of the dream of the botanical manuscript in his dream book. That is why, for instance, plants are so amenable to "letting themselves go," to losing a great number of their organs, returning them to the soil or rendering them fit for consumption, and then regenerating from that apparent loss. But, assuming that at the threshold of psychic life we find vegetal processes and faculties, this co-belonging of life and death is also at the roots of our unconscious.

When Freud "discovers" the death drive in *Beyond the Pleasure Principle*, he reaches a comparable conclusion, as a result of which "the theoretical importance of the instincts of self-preservation, of self-assertion and of mastery greatly diminishes" and the "guardians of life" appear as "the myrmidons of death" (SE 18: 39). Plants are here again at the forefront of de-rigidifying the boundaries of life and death. Against Wilhelm Fliess's notion of fixed and natural lifespans, Freud marshals the evidence gleaned from "certain large animals and certain gigantic arboreal growths [that] reach a very advanced age and one which cannot at present be computed." He adds: "When we see [. . .] how easily and how extensively the influence of external forces is able to modify the date of the appearance of vital phenomena (especially in the plant world)—to precipitate them or to hold them back—doubts must be cast upon the rigidity of Fliess's formulas" (SE 18: 45). While he raises these doubts, Freud does not contemplate the possibility that "external forces" are not so external from the standpoint of plants, which is to say that the difference between the inside and the outside melts away, as does, also, the one between life and death. The perdurance of other-than-human psychic structures and processes in the unconscious means that, subtending the hard and fast distinctions between life and death, the inside and the outside, self and other, are the fluid and permeable vegetal realities.

Q

Queer ecology, Freud-style

Throughout the book, I have been leaving various hints as to the queering of ecology and the psyche in Freudian psychoanalysis. It is now time to consolidate these clues, with a close reading of the first essay in *Three Essays on Sexuality*. In doing so, I will not concentrate on the second essay on infantile sexuality, since I have already registered the import of polymorphous perversity, discussed there, for the queering of sexuality and of ecology. Nor will I take up the third essay, "Transformations of Puberty," due to the limited scope of its applications.

In the first of *Three Essays* dealing with "sexual aberrations [*Abirrungen*]," Freud's goal is to show that these "aberrations" are very common and, in fact, nothing short of a norm. The scope of sexuality, after all, is much broader than that of reproduction: it encompasses pleasure and, under the ancient heading of *eros*, the cosmic force of assembling entities together. It is for this reason that Freud refuses to identify sexuality squarely with the biological or the cultural domains, with either "sexual needs" or "popular opinion" about these (SE 7: 135). Instead, he is interested in "sexual object" and "sexual aim" (SE 7: 136): to whom (or to what) sexual impulses are directed and for what purpose. Deviations and aberrations—the queering of sexuality—will be analyzed with respect to both objects and aims, without, at the same time, postulating an absolute object or aim.[1] Life is a more or less fortuitous, longer or shorter, series of detours toward death; sexuality, as Freud implies, is also a series of deviations moving toward a union with the sexual object, which, more or less metonymic, stands for the world at large.

Describing attraction to people of one's own sex ("inversion"), which pertains to modifications of the sexual object, Freud comes up with a provisional classification of "*absolute* inverts," "*amphigenic* inverts" (whom he also calls "psychosexual hermaphrodites"), and "*contingent* inverts" (SE 7: 136–7). Amphigenic inversion refers to bisexuality, which according to Freud's hypothesis is a default "universal" condition of all living beings, including humans (and, therefore, neither a deviation nor an aberration in the strict sense of these terms), while contingent inversion depends on "certain external conditions" that prompt people to treat members of their own sex as sexual objects. As these categories themselves show, human sexuality abuts the phenomena of plant sexuality (indeed, of other-than-human sexuality *tout court*) without being biologically deterministic. Plants and some animals (fish, gastropods, etc.) can also be sequentially or simultaneously hermaphroditic, while trees can develop male or female flowers, depending on the external circumstances. The *biological* plasticity of other-than-human sexuality becomes, between the lines of Freud's text, the *psychosexual* plasticity of human sexuality, queered with regard to its object choice, the constancy of that choice, and even speciation, assuming that strands of vegetal and animal life are discernible in it.

Freud accentuates the frequent inconstancy of object choice with reference to the question of time. The vectors of the libido are variable: "inversion" may "date back to the very beginning [. . .] or it may not have become noticeable till some particular time before or after puberty. It may either persist throughout life, or it may go into temporary abeyance [. . .]. It may even make its first appearance late in life after a long period of normal sexual activity. A periodic oscillation between a normal and an inverted sexual object has also sometimes been observed" (SE 7: 137). The queering of sexuality in time supplements its queering across species or biological kingdoms, intertwining in the human psyche. This emphasis on temporal instability and on "intermediate examples" (SE 7: 138) has the effect of de-essentializing Freud's take on sexuality, the effect buttressed by his rejection of physiological or biochemical theories of "nervous degeneracy" as the underlying cause of deviations.

Freud carves out the same niche for sexuality (which he analytically follows via its myriads of "deviations" and via countless variations on those) as for ecology—irreducible either to biology or to culture. Like ecology, sexuality is, in and of itself, queer, because it does not fit within established pairs of conceptual and epistemic oppositions. "We are therefore forced to a suspicion that the choice between 'innate' and 'acquired' is not an exclusive one or that it does not cover all the issues involved in inversion" (SE 7: 140).

Although Freud has Plato's *Symposium* in mind (a beautiful "poetic fable which tells how the original human beings were cut up into two halves—man and woman" [SE 7: 136]), the niche he carves out for sexuality and for queer ecology has more in common with another one of Plato's notions, namely *chôra* from *Timaeus*. Neither soul nor body, Plato's *chôra* is both, a "third kind," *triton genos*, or a third sex. *Chôra* is a "receptacle," that in which existence takes place, the place of place itself. Typically identified with the mother of life, s/he is not strictly sexuated and is, at the same time, the queering of ecology and of sex. The "third kind" comes first, or even before the first, as the material precondition for existence, much as in the "poetic fable" a third kind of human beings comes before the division into two sexes.

As for Freud, in *Three Essays*, he correlates "anatomical hermaphroditism" and "psychical hermaphroditism," faithful in all respects to the thinking of the "third kind." Moreover, Freud argues that the "rare cases" of babies born with both sets of genitals are merely accentuations of a prevalent tendency, taken to the extreme: "For it appears that a certain degree of anatomical hermaphroditism occurs normally. In every normal male or female individual, traces are found of the apparatus of the opposite sex. These either persist without function as rudimentary organs or become modified and take on other functions" (SE 7: 141). The queering of sexuality (hence, of psychic life as such) does not shirk the queering of anatomy. Note that Freud does not argue that psychical hermaphrodites are necessarily anatomical, or somatic, hermaphrodites (SE 7:142); rather, he thinks at the interface of the embodied mind and the enminded body, where the entire field of psychoanalysis unfolds. It is only necessary to add another interface between *this* interface and ecology, where sexual aims circulate, aims that are as outer as they are inner, actual and virtual, human and other-than-human.

In a footnote Freud will add to his 1905 work ten years later, he exhibits the most admirable open-mindedness, not only historicizing the normativity of sexual object choice, but also problematizing heteronormative sexuality. "Thus," he writes, "from the point of view of psychoanalysis, the exclusive sexual interest felt by men for women is also a problem that needs elucidating and is not a self-evident fact based upon an attraction that is ultimately of a chemical nature" (SE 7: 146). The idea is that to have such a rigid ("exclusive") sexual identity is to have practiced a great deal of severe repression. Could we not imagine the same sort of repression involved in the normalization and rigidification of an exclusively human identity that disregards the animal, vegetal, mineral, and other components (without a doubt imbued with strong libidinal significance) of our psychic and somatic composition? If so, it would not be sufficient to point out, diagnose, name the outcomes of this repression once and for all; repression and the defense mechanisms guaranteeing it tend to reconstitute themselves, requiring a patient and persistent analytic practice that contends, among other things, with the mechanisms of transference and countertransference.

In the course of considering the final aberration in sexual objects, which may include sexually immature persons and animals, Freud discovers in pedophilia and zoophilia (where "sexual attraction seems to override the barriers of species" [SE 7: 148]) an all-too-literal objectification of the instinct and its plasticity. Mindful of the fact that these practices are historically and circumstantially contingent, he compares, again in a later footnote, these *object choices*, proscribed in modernity, to the ancient valorization of the instinct over the object: "The most striking distinction between the erotic life of antiquity and our own no doubt lies in the fact that the ancients laid the stress upon the instinct itself, whereas we emphasize its object. The ancients glorified the instinct and were prepared on its account to honor even an inferior object; while we despise the instinctual activity in itself, and find excuses for it only in the merits of the object" (SE 7: 149). Freud stresses that, although "for us" instinctual activity must be justified, it is never justified on its own terms, but through an object and an aim deemed appropriate. To view sexuality on its own merits, prior to its distribution among different objects and aims, is to get in touch with its primary ecological queering, before the formalization of categories and purposes that arise along with particular kinds of objects and aims.

When it comes to "deviations in respect of the sexual aim," Freud shows how, even in the severely circumscribed field of genital sexuality that culminates in copulation, certain perversions are normalized and idealized in support of the overarching normative aim. So, "the kiss, one particular contact [...] between the mucous membrane of the lips of the two people concerned, is held in high sexual esteem among many nations [...] in spite of the fact that the parts of the body involved do not form part of the sexual apparatus but constitute the entrance to the digestive tract" (SE 7: 150). Elsewhere (including in another chapter of the present study), I have contemplated the kiss, extended beyond human practices to other species, biological kingdoms, and the world of the elements, as an alternative foundation for ecological being and knowing. It is the queering of sexuality and of the world—not to mention of physiological need, embodied in the digestive tract—which no longer serves its purpose, or which is endowed with ambiguous purposes, at loggerheads with one another.

In fact, the queering of sexuality has to do with the overriding of strict biological or anatomical purposes by troubling the correlations of specific organs or structures with their presumably default functions. The kiss reveals that the lips, the tongue, and the rest of the mouth are not only for eating (with the pun intended, tongue-in-cheek, Hegel has also made a dialectical discovery of speculatively contradictory activities of speaking and spitting centered on the same organs). Freud recalls that the genitals are organs of micturition (or urination) and of copulation, while rejecting disgust with anal sexuality as hysterical and extending the same duality to the anus (SE 7: 152). The open-ended multifunctionality of organs, in which the entire body of an organism and of the world is awash in sexuality, is prominent in the life of plants, where leaves, for example, are the organs of breathing, of nourishment, of photosensitivity (vision), hearing (via vibrations traveling through the air), and so forth. The queering of sexuality in the unfastening of exclusive sets of structures and functions from one another is of a piece with the queering of ecology, which proceeds in a vegetal key.

Far from endorsing as teleologically sound the pinnacle of sexuality in genital sexuality, Freud makes fun of its logic. If the only acceptable sexual aim is tethered to a given organ (here: the genitals), then it invites a libidinal approach toward the rest of the body of the partner as though it were a superfluous addition to that organ. To compensate for the truth of purely genital sexuality, the rest of the sexual object's body is "overvalued": from the genitals, "the appreciation extends to the whole body of the sexual object and tends to involve every sensation derived from it" (SE 7: 150). Overvaluation

(*Überschätzung*) then spreads further to "the psychological sphere: the subject becomes [...] intellectually infatuated" (SE 7: 150). But it is a very shoddy relation to the whole that, in a pervasive reaction formation, masks the devaluation of everything that is not genital with its opposite, overvaluation.

It is reasonable to conclude that every separation of a part (of a body, a mind, an interspecies assemblage, an ecosystem . . .) from the whole leads to the devaluation and reactive overvaluation of that whole. An individual subject, the human as such, each specimen or species taken separately is the culmination of the metaphysical parsing of the world in an analogous, if not a homologous, relation to genitals as the apex of all sexual striving and development. The wholes, in which these castrated parts belong, are devalued and subsequently hyper- or overvalued: much of the current "greening" of discourse and action is a symptom of just this overvaluation. The queering of sexuality and ecology implicit in Freud's writings would go a long way toward shifting libidinal dynamics from a mere reaction formation and fetishization to a vibrant, non-extractive energetic exercise of retying vital ties.

Here, we must pause for a moment, since our discussion elucidates afresh the notion of the fetish. We've already encountered the logic of the fetish as that of a substitute: "What is substituted for the sexual object is some part of the body (such as the foot or hair) which is in general very inappropriate for sexual purposes, or some inanimate object which bears an assignable relation to the person whom it replaces" (SE 7: 153). Nevertheless, the "sexual purposes" of genital sexuality are themselves very limited: they are substituted, à la fetish, for sexuality in general. One interpretative possibility is that those things that are called fetishes are the fetishes of a fetish. For my part, I prefer another interpretation, notably the idea that so-called fetishes are *less* of a fetish than the genitalia. In a roundabout way, the foot or hair or other body parts remind us of the sexualization of the entire body, and if this reminder bears the stamp of fetishism, that is because of the undue isolation and celebration of genital sexuality. *Mutatis mutandis*, the same logic is applicable to the other-than-human, environmental, or ecological fetishes: "pet causes," including the pets also known as "companion species;" ending the use of fossil fuels; the defense of the rainforest; or the inherently indeterminate "climate justice" are the partial reflections of anthropocentric fetishization.

A Freud-inspired queer ecology may begin with eco-fetishes, but it should not end there. The two pitfalls to avoid are the partial pet causes and an undifferentiated whole, such as Gaia. The queering of ecology is as stifled by hermetically sealed conceptual boxes, classing and classifying all beings, as it is by the amorphous and ultimately vacuous statements of total interconnectedness. More positively put, this queering is bound to pervasive tendencies, irrespective of systems of classification and strict structure–function correlations.

In my own work, I have pursued ecological queering by situating something of the vegetal in the human and in the growing-decaying ensemble of nature. I have also taken a hard look at the dump that suffuses all strata of being, confounding the distinctions among them, or at energy practices that are extractivist whenever they try to wrest potentialities from knowing subjects, from usable or valuable items, from the bowels of the earth, or from burning organic matter. How to respond to these overwhelming realities? My wager is this: by revitalizing surfaces (psychic, bodily, phenomenal, textual . . .) and interfaces without the fetish of depth; by allowing vitality to circulate, to be shared, and to grow thanks to the essentially superficial contacts among them.

R

Rats, horses, wolves, and other animals

Some of Freud's most famous clinical cases involve animals—a human patient's identification, obsession with, or fear of, rats, horses, wolves, and other participants in the psychoanalytic bestiary. Often, the phobia is that of being eaten or otherwise overpowered—including by a rat, a small animal, whom the patient known as Rat Man imagines biting and gnawing into his anus, based on an account of cruel torture. An ancient fear, it is imbued not only with sexual connotations (eating as the earliest, oral stage of sexuality, mixed with an anal fixation in the Rat Man), but also with the unmistakable alienation of Viennese city-dwellers from animal life and, indeed, from all life. If anything, this sense of alienation is still stronger in the twenty-first century, when there are no horse-drawn carriages, which played a crucial role in the case of Little Hans, on city streets, for example. And alienation from animal life outside oneself goes hand-in-hand with alienation from one's own animality, from the bodily functions and structures we share at least with other mammals.

Before turning to the details of these clinical cases, a few words are in order about animal activism. Undeniably important, demands for animal protection and respect for animal rights risk prematurely reconciling with the animals outside while still repressing the animal within one's psychophysical constitution. Alienation, after all, can assume a positive form, when it gives rise to insistence on respect (with the unbridgeable distance between the respecting and the respected put in place) or to a recognition of the other on the formal terrain of the bourgeois subject of rights, now broadened to include certain ecosystems and other entities granted personhood under the law. Similarly with an idealized construction of life, which forgets its inseparability from death, or from predator–prey relations in the animal world. Rather than empty soul-searching, a psychoanalytic examination of our relation to the undomesticated and indomitable "animality within" will only strengthen eco- and animal activists' formulations of their objectives and course of action.

As Oxana Timofeeva has pointed out in a recent study, all of Freud's patients suffering of what we might call "animal complexes" are men (or boys, as in the case of Little Hans); they are "Freud's beasty boys."[1] Little Hans, who developed an intense horse phobia, is exemplary in this regard.

With an early fixation on genitalia, linked at that age to the function of micturition, Little Hans is Freud's ideal sexual researcher child. Calling the genitals "widdler" (*Wiwimacher*), Hans seeks them everywhere, including an engine. Freud writes: "There can be no doubt about Hans's sexual curiosity; but it also roused the spirit of enquiry in him and enabled him to arrive at genuine abstract knowledge. When he was at the station once (at three and three-quarters) he saw some water being let out of the engine. 'Oh, look,' he said, 'the engine's widdling. Where's it got its widdler?' After a little he added in reflective tones: 'A dog and a horse have widdlers; a table and a chair haven't.' He had thus got hold of an essential characteristic for differentiating between animate and inanimate objects" (SE 10: 9). Needless to say, Freud overlooks the fact that this "essential characteristic" is applicable, in Hans's mind, to an engine or a hose as much as to a dog or a horse. This will be the first but not the last oversight on his part, probably due to countertransference and identification with his male patients.

A "widdler" becomes the principle of life, of animation—even if it is the life of a machine that is at stake. As a principle of life, it is not static, but itself growing: after seeing a giraffe at a zoo, Hans asks his father to draw the animal, and then to draw its widdler. "Draw it yourself," the father answers. Hans "began by drawing a short stroke, and then added a bit on to it, remarking: 'Its widdler's longer'" (SE 10: 13). An almost vegetal vitality animates the widdler in Hans's view, but what Freud again overlooks is that the boy identifies all genitalia with male genitalia, reducing female genitals and those who have them to the status of inanimate objects. This oversight is more serious than the first, and it will haunt the entire Little Hans case.

Later on, the boy will acknowledge the difference between male and female genitals, when observing his younger sister being bathed. This acknowledgment will be accompanied by laughter, indicating the inferiority of a girl's *Wiwimacher* compared to a boy's (SE 10: 21). But his relative sense of superiority is, at the same time, one of the triggers of phobia, to the extent that he realizes how his own penis is smaller than that of a horse: "The reason he was afraid of horses now was that he had taken so much interest in their widdlers" (SE 10: 28). The comparison of sizes and lengths is the beginning of hierarchical thinking, with strong fascist undertones: one feels superior to those who are lower down on the hierarchical ladder and inferior to, as well as fearful of, those who are higher up on the same ladder. A pastiche of animality and the very principle of life, of sexual difference and measures (length, size), the hierarchy Hans constructs in his mind is complex. It is not at all the case that the animal and the woman are grouped together on the lower end of the ladder: a horse is superior, while the sister is inferior. This realignment happens once the animal, too, is subsumed under the heading of masculinity, the horse representing the father, with whom Hans will have to identify in order to overcome his phobia and position himself at a higher hierarchical rank.

Little Hans's anxiety is, perhaps, less problematic from the political point of view than its fascist resolution. A "successful" overcoming of animal phobia, which is psychologically debilitating, leads to the consolidation of a society that is politically sick. Freud overlooks this factor, as well. "We may infer," he writes, "from his [Hans's] self-consolatory words ('my widdler will get bigger as I get bigger') that during his observations he had constantly been making comparisons, and that he had remained extremely dissatisfied with the size of his own widdler. Big animals reminded him of his defect, and were for that reason disagreeable to him. But since the whole train of thought was probably incapable of becoming clearly conscious, this distressing feeling, too, was transformed into anxiety" (SE 10: 35).

In the case of the Rat Man, a "great obsessive fear" is triggered by an account of torture "used in the East," in which "the criminal was tied up," "a pot was turned upside down on his buttocks," "some *rats* were put into it" and "*bored their way in*[to]" his anus (SE 10: 166). Freud's patient invokes the "idea" (which Freud interprets as an unconscious wish) that this torture would be applied to two people who are dear to him—his fiancée and his already deceased father (SE 10: 167). Here, the entire small animal metonymically represents the phallus, while its interaction with the human body assumes the shape of "*anal eroticism*" (SE 10: 213), though Freud confesses that the symbolic meanings associated with the rat were multiple and unstable. Among these, Freud isolates money and infection, given that "rats are carriers of dangerous infectious diseases" (SE 10: 214). And here another instant of inattentiveness discloses Freud's own bias.

Rat Man hears the story about the cruel torture using rats as instruments from his army commander, who mentions that the original context of its deployment is "in the East." This is not a trivial detail, but the glue, holding sundry bits of the case's unconscious cluster together. "The East" is coded here as the region of human inhumanity, of unspeakable cruelty (which, nevertheless, is also proper to the Rat Man, beneath the veneer of his disgust). As a whole, it comes to be embodied in the animal figure of the rat—sexualized, yet considered dirty, a carrier of infections, desirable and dangerous, always prepared to infiltrate (the anus, "the West," etc.). The main traits of Edward Said's Orientalism are visible in this set of unconscious associations, whose logic escapes both Freud and his patient. Added to the Orientalist gist of the story is Freud's casual remark about "intercourse *per anum*" and "certain curses in use among the Southern Slavs" that have to do with "arse-fucking" (SE 10: 214–15, 311). Clearly, the Slavs appear as an intermediate link between "the East" and "the West," thereby substantiating the unconscious cluster in question.

The twist is that the Orientalized, animalized Other is actually a part of oneself, which has become split off and dissociated, unacceptable as it is to the superego. So, Rat Man is both horrified by rats and empathizes with them, becoming at the level of his psychic life a real hybrid, part rat and part human. "But rats cannot be sharp-toothed, greedy and dirty with impunity: they are cruelly persecuted and mercilessly put to death by man, as the patient had often observed with horror. He had often enough pitied the poor creatures. But he himself had been just such a nasty, dirty little wretch, who was apt to bite people when he was in a rage, and had been fearfully punished for doing so" (SE 10: 216). As an unconscious subject, one is foreign to oneself: the mystified, repellant, and attractive East is in the West and the West *is* the East. Interspecies hybridity dovetails with intercultural amalgamation.

The episodes of his empathy toward and faint self-recognition in rats do not redeem Rat Man. It is through cruelty to oneself that one is cruel to the animal and racialized Other. Empathy merely puts into relief the cycle of torments, in which the original story of torture *with* rats is mirrored by the torturing *of* rats: "He saw them catching rats and heard that they threw them into the boiler" (SE 10: 289–90). Within this cycle, the goal is not to escape torture but to become a torturer oneself, to occupy the place of the father: "Other stories of cruelty followed, which finally centered on his father. The sight of the cat gave him the idea that his father was in the sack. When his father was serving with the army, corporal punishment was still in force. He described how he had once and once only, in a fit of temper, struck a recruit with the butt-end of his rifle, and he had fallen down" (SE 10: 290). If, following one train of associations, children are rats, then rat torture is supposed to be their revenge against the father (cat), including, symbolically, after his death, even as former children become cats toward their own rat children.

In the case of the Wolf Man, whose childhood neurosis is analyzed by Freud when the patient is a young adult, extreme fear of wolves, similarly to Rat Man, coincides with the fear of and cruelty toward other animals, "big and little." In spite of being scared of a butterfly the boy was chasing, he "could remember that at this very time he used to torment beetles and cut caterpillars to pieces" (SE 17: 16). Freud surmises that a threat of castration, issued by the governess, resulted in a sadistic-anal character of the Wolf Man who "became irritable and a tormentor, and gratified himself in this way at the expense of animals and humans" (SE 17: 26). The main takeaway message of the case, however, is not the rather banal point about the externalization of internalized violence, but about the concentration of the fear of animals in the figure of the wolf, who is an "anxiety-animal" not "easily accessible to observation (such as a horse or a dog), but [. . .] known to him only from stories and picture-books" (SE 17: 32). So, why the wolf?

Everything revolves around a dream, in which, in the patient's words, "suddenly the window opened of its own accord, and I was terrified to see that some white wolves were sitting on the big walnut tree in front of the window.

There were six or seven of them. The wolves were quite white, and looked more like foxes or sheep-dogs, for they had big tails like foxes and they had their ears pricked like dogs when they pay attention to something" (SE 17: 29). Freud interprets the dream as the primal scene, the windows being the young boy's eyes that open to what he experiences as the violent event of his parents having sexual intercourse. The immobility of the wolves is supposed to signify his own paralysis in the face of the unprecedented scene (SE 17: 35), which he can only associate with an animal "not easily accessible to observation." Freud goes so far as to conjecture the poses the parents assumed during their coitus: "the man upright, and the woman bent down like an animal," which is significant, given that the picture provoking the most fear in Wolf Man was of a wolf "shown standing upright, with one foot forward, with its claws stretched out and its ears pricked" (SE 17: 39).

There are several inconsistencies in the interpretation. First, although the wolves on a tree are Wolf Man himself, observing the primal scene, the scene itself includes the terrifying wolf, who is the father. The process of identification will not have taken place yet, implying that the wolf cannot be the observer and the observed at the same time. Second, Freud drops various hints that the wolf could represent the mother, in light of the fairy tales "Little Red Riding-Hood" and "The Wolf and the Seven Little Goats": in the former, the wolf passes himself for the grandmother; in the latter, when the little goats are rescued, the wolf's belly is cut to release them, recalling the event of birth (SE 17: 31). It follows that the wolf is the boy, the father, and the mother—actually, *everyone*. Third, the wolves on the tree are many, rather than two (parents) or one (child). Freud accounts for this discrepancy by resorting to the unconscious transformation of the memory of the primal scene, in which "the *two* parents [are] to be replaced, as was desirable, by *several* wolves" (SE 17: 42). In their rebuke to Freud, Deleuze and Guattari recall that, for the psychoanalyst himself, the wolves are the observer child, who is already a pack, the multitude of the unconscious irreducible to the One, a rhizome, a molecular plurality.[2] Still, something else is missing from this list of inconsistencies, many of them fecund. That something is disregard for species boundaries.

The logic of a dream by and large trespasses on all kinds of boundaries, but here the trespass is imbued with extra significance. The wolves on a tree are said to be reminiscent of foxes, due to their fluffy tails, of dogs, due to their pricked ears, and (this goes unmentioned) of little goats, due to their white color and ability to climb trees. Their composite image combines predator and prey, father and mother and child, the observer and the observed. The wolf is everyone, but *the wolf is not a wolf*, which is probably why s/he can stand for everyone. The primal scene is that of life before its compartmentalization into distinct species—an untamed, unclassifiable life that permeates the rest of the narrative. Wolf Man's infantile neurosis is an overreaction to this looseness, an attempt to impose immutable boundaries onto the mixtures, hybrids, and other mélanges of different beings and primal scenes: not the least of life's primal scene.

S

Sadism and the sentience of other-than-human beings

I propose to start this chapter with a true story. In Spring 2012, I published an op-ed in the *New York Times*, titled "If Peas Can Talk, Should We Eat Them?"[1] The title, to be sure, was proposed by the *NYT* editor. My original suggestion was "Ethics and the Pea," playfully alluding to Hans Christian Andersen's fairy tale "The Princess and the Pea" and *problematizing* ethical hypersensitivity that comes with the privileged status of the ethicists themselves, a little like the hypersensitivity of the princess who felt discomfort when she slept on top of a pea covered by a huge pile of soft mattresses. The substitute title did not faithfully reflect the article, but it did achieve the desired scandalous effect, also because many readers didn't seem to have read the text that followed it. Among hateful online commentaries written in response to the piece, several stood out for their gratuitous cruelty. For example: "I have never read such nonsense in my life. Now I'm going out to pull weeds. I think I'll torture them a little, too." Or: "My split-pea soup tastes all the sweeter now that I know the peas were screaming in pain as they were being boiled."

The obviously sadistic sentiment of these comments is not an aberration; it furnishes a point of access to age-old attitudes toward "nature" as something to be mastered, dominated, subjugated, subdued, where the affective surplus-value of such behavior is sadistic satisfaction. While the early works of eco-feminism (e.g., Val Plumwood) and of Frankfurt School critical theorists (Horkheimer and Adorno) have noted this connection, a Freud-inspired approach has the potential of fleshing it out and, above all, of showing the hidden complicity between the sadistic treatment of life as such and its masochistic inversion.

Since the first detailed discussions of sadism in *Three Essays on Sexuality* (1905), Freud insisted on the pairing of sadism with masochism, stating that "the most remarkable feature of this perversion is that its active and passive forms are habitually found to occur together in the same individual [...] A sadist is always at the same time a masochist, although the active or the passive aspect of the perversion may be the more strongly developed in him and may represent his predominant sexual activity" (SE 7: 159). Whereas sadism involves not only violence toward its object but also "satisfaction [that] is entirely conditional on the humiliation and maltreatment of the object" (SE 7: 158), the masochist underside of sadists is contingent upon their experiences of being humiliated and maltreated. Sadism toward other-than-human nature contains an unconscious trace of being maltreated and humiliated by *it*, by the overwhelming force of the waves and of hurricanes, of extreme heat or cold, of wild carnivorous animals in the woods or poisonous plants and mushrooms.

In the 1915 metapsychological study, "Instincts and Their Vicissitudes," Freud will postulate the principle responsible for the coexistence of the opposites—sadism and masochism—even within the same individual. The key is, precisely, the "vicissitudes," or the "destinies" (*Schicksale*) of instincts, which rarely, if ever, reach their aims directly. One of their main "destinies" is reversal: "Reversal of an instinct into its opposite resolves on closer examination into two different processes: a change from activity to passivity, and a reversal of its content" (SE 14: 127). The idea is that masochists are, at one and the same time, sadists toward themselves.[2] "The turning round of an instinct upon the subject's own self," Freud continues, "is made plausible by the reflection that masochism is actually sadism turned round upon the subject's own ego" (SE 14: 127).

With regard to a sadistic attitude to other-than-human nature, we are now witnessing, on the one hand, the entrenchment of this attitude and behavior by climate change deniers and proponents of the limitless exploitation of "natural resources" and, on the other, its reversal into a masochist position, in the sense that humanity is dumber than many species, that it *should* be extinct and that it deserves all the disastrous consequences of climate change and of the destruction of the biosphere. The rational argument that "humanity" is too broad a category, which fails to take into account regional, class, gender, and generational differences in contributing to the current predicament pales in comparison with the outpouring of instinct that, in its vicissitudes, is reversed into masochism. Despite the change of object, "the aim remains unchanged" (SE 14: 127), namely "the enjoyment of pain [that] would thus be an aim which was originally masochistic, but which can only become an instinctual aim in someone who was originally sadistic" (SE 14: 128).

Lest we forget, the "subject's own *ego*" that is now on the receiving end of sadistic comportment is an *eco*-subject, an essentially intermediary, middle term slotted between the inner demands of the unconscious and the outer world. All manners of reversal are intensified with regard to the ego, because its own position is ambivalent (neither inner nor outer *and* both). Freud actually adopts Bleuler's term "ambivalence" to refer to "the opposing pairs of instinct [...] developed to an approximately equal extent" (SE 7: 199), particularly when it comes to activity and passivity in the sadomasochist vicissitudes of instincts: "The desire to torture has turned into self-torture and self-punishment [...] The active voice is changed, not into the passive, but into the reflexive, the middle voice" (SE 14: 128). The middle—for instance, the ego, not as a psychic container but as the intermediary—is a time and a place propitious to reversals, inherently unstable and ambivalent. But a similar change also takes place in the turn from "nature" to "ecology," as a result of which the ego is viewed (and perceives itself) as a middle in the middle. The reversal of instinct is stronger and more indeterminate in these circumstances. The ecological sense of the ego is, then, likely to contribute to a more violent movement of the instinctual swing.

In his treatment of sadism and masochism—and still before his focus on the death drive in *Beyond the Pleasure Principle*—Freud highlights the affects of love/hate and the aims of mastery/subjection, with the psychological supplements of humiliation, pain, and suffering that ultimately override these aims. In *Three Essays on Sexuality*, he writes: "Cruelty in general comes easily to the childish nature, since the obstacle that brings the instinct for mastery to a halt at another person's pain—namely a capacity for pity—is developed relatively late. The fundamental psychological analysis of this instinct has, as we know, not yet been satisfactorily achieved. It may be assumed that cruelty arises from the instinct for mastery and appears at a period of sexual life at which the genitals have not yet taken over their later role" (SE 7: 192–3). Such pitiless cruelty is symptomatic of the sadist's indifference to the destruction of the object, toward which the instinct has been unleashed. When it is conventionally impermissible to exhibit this attitude to other people, it may be transferred onto other forms of life, including pea plants in the story, with which I opened this chapter.

Indifferent cruelty has, by definition, no admixed hatred; in fact, Freud claims that "it is also through the medium of this connection between libido and cruelty that the transformation of love into hate takes place, the transformation of affectionate into hostile impulses, which is characteristic of a great number of cases of neurosis" (SE 7: 167). The default position of libidinal life here is love, which, by means of the desire to master the outside world and the indifferent cruelty in acting upon this desire, is reversed into hate. In "Instincts and Their Vicissitudes," Freud, nonetheless, reverses the reversal of love and hate instincts: "Indeed, it may be asserted that the true prototypes of the relation of hate are derived not from sexual life, but from the ego's struggle to preserve and maintain itself [. . .] Hate, as a relation to objects, is older than love [. . .] When the ego-instincts dominate the sexual function, as is the case at the stage of the sadistic-anal organization, they impart the qualities of hate to the instinctual aim as well" (SE 14: 138–9).

Obviously, the vicissitudes of instincts are far from unidirectional. They swing both ways: from love to hate and from hate to love. But why does Freud seem to contradict himself on the *primacy* of hate in psychic life?

I would suggest that the apparent contradiction has to do with the parallax view of the ego itself, as it is formulated, at times explicitly and at other times implicitly, in Freud's body of thought. The counterweight to libidinal economy in psychoanalysis is not so much the dynamic and topographical views of the psyche, but libidinal ecology, where, as we have seen, THE EGO IS ECO. According to the economic model, the ego is a kind of psychic container; its main goal is to preserve itself, to master the other, to eat up and assimilate the other, and to enhance the chances of self-preservation by means of this very mastery. In this paradigm, "hate, as a relation to objects," is really "older than love." According to the ecological model, the ego is nothing but a psychosomatic membrane, the in-between time and space of the psyche juggling the oft-incompatible demands of the instincts and external reality or of different parts of the psyche itself. Here, love is primary not in the sense of merging with the rest of the world, on the model of the oceanic feeling, but as a series of jointures, of assemblages and reconciliations, however fleeting. The "middle voice" of the eco-ego does not, for all that, overcome the challenge of sadism: it swings to the other side, transforming hate into love in a masochistic (and somewhat Christian) manner. The contemporary love of the earth, love of nature, of animals and plant life is saddled with this heavy unconscious baggage, as well.

With the inclusion of Thanatos alongside Eros as the other fundamental unconscious instinct in *Beyond the Pleasure Principle*, Freud will hypothesize that "there might be such a thing as primary masochism" (SE 18: 55). Nevertheless, letting go of oneself as a definite unit of identity, which is one of the aims of the death drive, may be interpreted as masochist only on the condition that the egoic sense of self is a priori sadist—a container to be maintained and preserved almost exclusively through mastery and domination over others. Libidinal ecology, anticipated but not formulated in Freud's works, requires taking a view at the psyche, the instincts, affects, and so on from the middle, rather than from the extremes, from the vicissitudes, the times-places of incessant reversal, inversion, and perversion constitutive of psychic life, rather than from its reversed, inverted, and perverted contents.

Assuming that one adheres to a strictly economic view of the libido, masochism (which subverts the sadist aspiration to self-preservation via domination) is an aporia, or at least a problem. Freud expresses this insight in the title of his 1924 essay, "The Economic Problem of Masochism," and immediately goes on to qualify this problem as "mysterious" (SE 19: 159), seeing that masochism signals a sort of paralysis of the pleasure principle. "In the service of the death instincts," masochism would be suicidal (SE 19: 160). (But isn't sadism, above all the ecological permutation of sadism, still more suicidal in its destruction of life and its support systems than the masochism that only threatens to eliminate the masochist him- or herself?) It yields no returns on psychic investment, unless those returns are purely negative. So why does masochism persist, not as an occasional aberration, but as a constant of libidinal development, in an arc stretching from "the fear of being eaten up by the totem animal (father)" to castration anxiety (SE 19: 165)?

The answer hinges on the moral variety of masochism: through guilt and self-punishment, this masochism is an upshot of the sadistic superego. "The superego—the conscience at work in the ego—may [...] become harsh, cruel and inexorable against the ego which is in its charge. Kant's Categorical Imperative is thus the direct heir of the Oedipus complex" (SE 19: 167). With guilt-ridden environmental brooding and activism, we get a reflexive reversal of ecological sadism; with the heedless destruction of a livable world, limitless drilling for oil, deforestation, burning of fossil fuels, and so on, sadism *proper* holds sway. Although they belong to the extreme ends of the ideological-political spectrum, the two forms of sadism coexist, feed off one another, and populate the universe of psychological one-dimensionality—to recycle Herbert Marcuse's diagnosis from the 1960s.

Succinctly put, the economic problem (of masochism, and not only) is how a phenomenon lends a voice to its opposite, whereas the ecological conundrum is that of the opposites merging in the middle. Freud famously traces the sadistic superego to strict parental authority, which is gradually detached from the actual figures of the parents. This detachment is never complete, however; Freud sees in it a series of replacements: "all who transfer the guidance of the world to Providence, to God, or to God and Nature, arouse a suspicion that they still look upon these ultimate and remotest powers as a parental couple, in a mythological sense, and believe themselves linked to them by libidinal ties" (SE 19: 168). Nature understood in this way is yet another replacement of a punishing parental figure, both externalized in being projected onto the world at large and internalized as the sadistic superego. Its corollary is a masochistic ego, in that "the sadism of the superego and the masochism of the ego supplement each other and unite to produce the same effects" (SE 19: 170)—here, of a masochistic acceptance (and perhaps enjoyment) of disasters said to be natural.

Having departed from the overt displacement of sadism onto plants as sentient beings, we have reached the covert sadism of the masochist stance, assumed by large swathes of eco-activism and veganism, not to mention the many Western critics of the Anthropocene and post-colonialism. Freud treats moral masochism as evidence for the "fusion of instinct," where Eros and Thanatos converge. His warning is probably starker now than it was a century ago, at the time of the essay's composition: the danger of moral masochism "lies in the fact that it originates from the death instinct and corresponds to the part of that instinct which has escaped being turned outwards as an instinct of destruction. But since, on the other hand, it has the significance of the erotic component, even the subject's destruction of himself cannot take place without libidinal satisfaction" (SE 19: 170).

T

Trauma extensions

The first thing to note is that trauma is not synonymous with an injury (psychological or physical), severe damage, and the like. These may be its efficient causes and effects, but trauma itself, in the psychoanalytic sense of the term, is irreducible to them; it is in excess of representational and calculative capacities, not least because, often enough, it irrupts before these capacities have been developed in the course of individual lifetime.

In *Moses and Monotheism*, Freud defines trauma as follows: "We give the name of *traumas* to those impressions, experienced early and later forgotten, to which we attach such great importance in the etiology of the neuroses" (SE 23: 72). Traumatic impressions are not processed by the apparatus of consciousness, either because this apparatus is not yet developed and equipped to deal with them or because they overwhelm the limited resources of conscious life, its perceptual and cognitive limits, its defenses and other mental banisters. That is why the impressions remain intact—though it seems that they are forgotten—and, indigestible within individual psychic life, spawn a welter of effects, chief among them neuroses and the related compulsion to repeat, returning time and again to the source of trauma, circling around it, bereft of the means to deal with this non-experience in an alternative way.

Within a few pages of *Moses and Monotheism*, Freud details the mechanisms of trauma and its aftermath with remarkable concision. Traumatic impressions yield positive and negative reactions, notably fixations and phobias. Fixations drive the compulsion to repeat, obviating any sort of resolution. Phobias and inhibitions are, in turn, defensive reactions that divert attention from the source of trauma (SE 23: 73–6). While fixations and phobias impose incompatible demands on the ego, the role of the latter is to negotiate a compromise solution between these positive and negative repercussions of trauma. The outbreak of neurotic illness is a sign of ego failure, the impasse reached in the task of finding a workable solution in the long run, leading, after a phase of latency, to the "partial return of the repressed" (SE 23: 80).

Freud's emphasis on childhood trauma goes back to his studies with Charcot and with Breuer (SE 14: 17), even though Freud replaces hypnotic techniques for lifting the veil of repression and getting to the bottom of trauma with his strategy of free association. He is also influenced by (and, in "Analysis Terminable and Interminable," reacts rather harshly against) Otto Rank's 1924 study, *The Trauma of Birth*, which traces "the true source of neurosis" to "the act of birth, since this involves the possibility of a child's 'primal fixation' to his mother not being surmounted but persisting as a 'primal repression'" (SE 23: 216). Rank's work, which merits detailed study in its own right, takes trauma to its earliest and widest locus: birth is the child's separation from the mother's body and, as such, it is an event shared with everyone who is born, whether human or not. The trigger of trauma is expulsion from the protected intrauterine environment, ejection into a threatening outside world. Taking into account the sense of nature as birth (via the Latin verb *nasci*, "to be born," and its past participle *natus*),[1] Rank's thesis means that nature itself is not only traumatized; nature *is* trauma, reenacted with every new birth.

The historical bearings of this speculative thesis on the twenty-first century hardly need elaboration. The geological epoch of the Anthropocene receives its specific identity from the production, release, and storage (including in geological crusts) of materials that do not decompose, or decompose so slowly as to be all but immutable within the worlds they clog. Micro- and nanoplastics saturating every milieu and organismic tissues are the physical instantiations of trauma as that which is indigestible, or non-metabolizable, in individual organisms, in the elements, and in ecosystems. Nuclear waste and the radioactive isotopes left over from technogenic disasters and weapon testing are, similarly, the material and ecological facets of trauma, alongside the "forever chemicals" and other indissoluble toxic substances.

I am not citing these well-known examples by way of an analogy or as a metaphor of psychological trauma "applied" (in fact, applications are also a matter of extension—that is, of extending a certain logic to instances not initially contemplated by it) to the plane of life systems, ecosystems, and the planet.[2] Rather, the same sweeping tendency of traumatization, which I have elsewhere termed "dumpification,"[3] affects every region of existence, so much so that it becomes the name for being in the twenty-first century.

The connection of non-decomposable materials to trauma is at least double: 1) the non-metabolizable nature of these materials themselves, and 2) our relation to them. It is worth sifting through this traumatic overlay in order to begin surveying the various senses of ecological trauma.

If traumas are impressions that cannot be erased or transformed without considerable analytic effort, then "in themselves" they are the permanent marks left on landscapes and bodies, on the ecosystemic and organismic *places* that are traumatized along with, and as, the psyche. These are impressions that, while static or barely changing, keep spawning multiple effects—for instance, on DNA replication, cell reproduction, soil composition, and modes of behaving—even under the cover of repression, hidden under further layers of the earth or of mental representations. To say that places (such as Chernobyl or Fukushima, the land and the ocean and the air above them ...) are traumatized is to invert the Freudian notion of *the topography of mental life*, most memorably compared to the city of Rome in *Civilization and Its Discontents*. Here, we are dealing with *the mental life of a topography* at every conceivable scale, from the microscopic to the planetary and the cosmic.

As we have seen, the two main responses to the trauma are fixation and inhibition/phobia, and they, too, transpire on two levels. Fixation is the fixity of materials that persist in the milieu they have been released into; inhibition is the tendency of these same materials to reduce the possibilities of a flourishing life all around them, while also standing in the way of a different, fertile future. The fixity of being that is inimical to becoming is, actually, the ideal of Western metaphysics, from Plato's Ideas onward. This means that metaphysics is trauma hypostatized and idealized, exhibiting a strong fixation on the unchangeable, grasped as true being, and a phobia/inhibition of matter, decay, time, and becoming. The self-aggrandizing "highest achievement" of thought is an acting out of the unconscious as such, instead of this or that unconscious reaction. For all its fetishization of objective, universal truth, metaphysics qua trauma is the brainchild of the id: "There is nothing in the id that corresponds to the idea of time; there is no recognition of the passage of time, and [...] no alteration in its mental processes is produced by the passage of time [...] Impressions, too, which have been sunk into the id by repression are virtually immortal; after the passage of decades, they behave as though they had just occurred" (SE 22: 74). At times, Freud was taken to task for a nearly metaphysical notion of the unconscious he formulates in passages such as this one. But, to turn the tables on the usual critique, do not virtually all metaphysical genuine "realities" behave in the manner of the Freudian unconscious, to the extent to which they are oblivious to the passage of time even after millennia have elapsed?

As a planet-wide trauma, the environmental crisis is a point of fixation, in which all other social, political, and economic problems are anchored, and a point of inhibition, diverting attention from the source of trauma to the need to ensure economic growth, for instance, or to balance ecological realities with economic exigencies. The most extreme form of inhibition is "climate change denial," which, by way of negating change, affirms the stuckness of trauma itself. But inhibitions can also vaguely acknowledge the problem in the atmosphere of a paralyzing fear in the face of the impact, immensity, and finality of the traumatic event. To eco-anxiety, we ought to add eco-phobias (yet to be catalogued). The compromise solution is the disavowal of the environmental crisis, with annual global climate summits taking place under the auspices of top oil-producing countries. Evidently, the compromise solution is unworkable; it paves the way to the return of the repressed in the shape of multiple manifestations of the climate catastrophe around the globe.

Repetition compulsion, which is the neurotic response to trauma instigated by fixation, is the stubborn reassertion of and clinging to the source of the problem, perhaps under different guises. In the history of metaphysics, repetition compulsion is palpable in the constant renaming of the true unchangeable being (trauma) as Ideas, the unmoved mover, God, substance, subject, Spirit, and so forth. In variegated responses to the environmental crisis, this compulsion repeats the very logic, replete with technological spinoffs, that has led to the crisis in the first place, be it through insistence on the same mode of energy production (just "cleaner") or through the resolve to come up with technological solutions to technogenic problems. With regard to metaphysics, internal trauma yielding a manner of thinking and its fantastic, phantasmatic projections to the realm of true being, cannot be worked through without addressing the traumas of bodies, places, and worlds; with respect to the environmental crisis, the external trauma of the planet cannot be worked through without paying close attention to the internal trauma of cognition, the rules and expectations attached to reasoning, the epistemologies and fixed/fixated formal methods that inhibit a thinking relation to life. In sum, what we are witnessing is a traumatic, traumatized and traumatizing, response to trauma, the latency of which is as unsustainable as compromise Band-Aid solutions proposed by the ego.

In the 1938 text, *An Outline of Psychoanalysis*, Freud suggests that the source of trauma may itself be external or internal. "Instinctual demands from within," he writes, "no less than excitations from the external world, operate as 'traumas', particularly if they are met halfway by certain innate dispositions" (SE 23: 185). And, Freud adds, "no human individual is spared such traumatic experiences; none escapes the repressions to which they give rise" (SE 23: 185).

The universality of trauma and the way it breaches the metaphysical boundaries between the inside and the outside support our thesis about its ecological and material extensions beyond the realm of the human psyche. Granting that ecosystems are as traumatized as the individual psyche is admitting that other-than-human beings are also the bearers of trauma. The pre-linguistic and pre-symbolic stage of traumatization is important: in animals and plants, fungi and bacteria, traumatic impressions wreak havoc similar to the one they cause in a human infant, unable to put these experiences or non-experiences into words. Nevertheless, if every form of life has a language, or, better, if every form of life *is* a language, tentatively understood as a mode of expression and communication put to the task of interpreting its lifeworld and its inner states, then, in other-than-human beings, trauma does not remain confined to the pure materiality of organismic existence. The "resilience" of ecosystems, the plants' impressive capacity to deal with and, to a certain extent, neutralize heavy metals and radioactive isotopes, the resurgence of life in the most hostile of environments are all modes of working through trauma, often more effectively than either human individuals or collectivities are capable of doing.

Freud's assertion about early trauma, which coincides with the condition of being human before learning to verbalize and symbolize existence, refers not only to individual infancy but also to the infancy of the human species, the "prehistory" of "the human race" (SE 23: 80). The correlation between individual and species development, which Freud establishes throughout his work, is reflected in correspondences and resonances among different levels and scales of trauma. Taking the idea of scales seriously, we may amend Freud's notes: when he writes that "the operative and forgotten traumas relate to life in the human family" (SE 23: 80), we may insist that they are, more broadly, related to life in the planetary family.

To Freud, the temporal correlation affords a more flexible approach to the veracity of traumatic events, as far as their unfolding in the life of the traumatized subject is concerned. Since trauma is an "*archaic heritage*" (SE 23: 98), it need not be an event that actually befell this subject: "When we study the reactions to early traumas, we are quite often surprised to find that they are not strictly limited to what the subject himself has really experienced but diverge from it in a way which fits in much better with the model of a phylogenetic event" (SE 23: 99). In "On the History of the Psychoanalytic Movement," Freud is blunter still: "If hysterical subjects trace back their symptoms to traumas that are fictitious, then the new fact which emerges is precisely that they create such scenes in *phantasy*, and this psychical reality requires to be taken into account alongside practical reality" (SE 14: 17–18). To us, the traversal of different scales of traumatized being, from the atomic to the planetary, means that one may treat as one's own the trauma of Chernobyl or Fukushima, the trauma of a place and its inhabitants, without having "really experienced" it. This is what is also at stake in the so-called generational trauma, let alone a planet where traumatized places grow exponentially, often with tentacular links developing among them.

Comparing the etiologies of neurotic disturbance where trauma is predominant with those where excessively strong instinctual demands are the lead factor, Freud is more optimistic about the success of analytic work in the former scenario (namely, the traumatic one): "Only when a case is a predominantly traumatic one will analysis succeed in doing what it is so superlatively able to do; only then will it, thanks to having strengthened the patient's ego, succeed in replacing by a correct solution the inadequate decision made in his [the patient's] early life" (SE 23: 220). To cure a neurotic disturbance, the analysand must have at least a minimal awareness of the problem, the very awareness that is absent when the predominant etiology of neurosis is a heedless quest for pleasure. The energy solutions and those linked to sustainable development that are being sought nowadays must be, in line with this argument, psychological solutions arising from the arduous process of working through the eco-traumas of the twentieth and twenty-first centuries. Conversely, the purely technological and technocratic solutions are nothing but expressions of traumatic symptomatology, of fixations and avoidances.

So, the traumatic backdrop of neurotic breakdowns is more promising for dealing with the problem of ego failure than the unfulfillable demands of the id. The desires associated with unbridled consumerism, the extraction and burning of energy at any price, the illusion of the non-depletable abundance of renewable materials, and the unshakable conditions of possibility for future life—all these are not as amenable to change as traumatization, gradually replaced by "a correct solution" to the crisis. But it is far from certain that the same psycho-techno-cratic strategy will be successful in caring for and curing traumatized places, materials, or ecosystems.

Freud points to the consequences of the dire efforts to achieve wish fulfillment in the shadow of trauma in the case of recurrent nightmarish dreams: "People who have experienced a shock, a severe psychological trauma, [. . .] are regularly taken back in their dreams into the traumatic situation." But, Freud continues, "according to our hypothesis about the function of dreams this should not occur. What wishful impulse could be satisfied by harking back in this way to this exceedingly distressing traumatic experience?" (SE 22: 28). The answer is that "the function of the dream has failed" (SE 22: 29). Such dreams are attempts to fulfill the wish of an escape from traumatic fixations, but they rush headlong to the very thing they were meant to escape from. The ideological dreams that are dreamt in a wide-awake state today replicate these dynamics. Dystopias and post-apocalyptic visions of the unlivable world are not tools for contending with eco-trauma; they are, precisely, the fixated and inhibiting nightmarish visions that betray the failure of wish fulfillment—wishing the actual nightmare of a traumatized world *away*.

Sometimes, failed wish fulfillment gives off the impression of a happy end. When Chernobyl, the site of the worst nuclear disaster on earth, is proclaimed a success story, given the impressive resurgence of plant and animal life in the area, what stays in the shadows is the lingering effect of radiation that keeps provoking genetic mutations and destroying the fragile communities of decomposers, including fungi, bacteria, and other microorganisms. Any future growth is, as a result, unsustainable there, because of the unpassing present of nuclear trauma, which impedes soil renewal; radiation literally fixes and fixates the soil and organic matter in a state of perpetual being without becoming, even as it instigates relatively fast changes, all the way down to the molecular and genetic levels, that amount to a becoming without becoming. Dream-work "would like to transform the memory-traces of the traumatic event into the fulfilment of a wish" (SE 22: 29), and it is this feigned transformation that is celebrated around Chernobyl, while nuclear memory-traces in the soil and the rest of the milieu keep reenacting an *extended* trauma. It is high time to wake up and to realize that the end is not a happy one and that, indeed, it is not quite an end, in light of the lasting effects of extremely radioactive materials, with which the place is suffused. A theory of the more-than-human trauma is a baby step in the process of such an awakening.

U

Uncanniness: leaving, coming back home, and leaving again with ecology

Much has been written on the subject of the uncanny in literary studies, with an eye to the semantic texture of the German term Freud uses. *Unheimlich* means "unhomely," but it is a strangeness permeating what is otherwise habitual. The uncanny does not then mean not being at home outside one's home, but rather not being at home right here, *at home*, in the midst of apparent familiarity, in the interlocked domains of habit, habituation, and habitat.

One reason for bringing the uncanny to the conceptual and affective vicinities of ecology is that the latter term also circles around home, the Greek *oikos* that forms one of its parts (*eco-*). More than that, the "invention" of ecology in the nineteenth century coincided with the time when the feeling of being at home in the world was quickly eroded due to rapid industrialization and urbanization. Ecology, therefore, bears uncanniness as its birthmark.

Prior to his extensive treatment of the subject of the uncanny in a homonymous 1919 essay, Freud occasionally mentions it in discussions of obsessive wishes and fears. In 1909, in what must have been the earliest invocation of the term, Freud comments on a case of childhood obsessional neurosis: "To find a chronic obsessional neurosis beginning like this in early childhood, with lascivious wishes of this sort connected with uncanny apprehensions and an inclination to the performance of defensive acts, is no new thing to me" (SE 10: 165). Referencing "uncanny apprehensions," Freud resorts (unconsciously, uncannily?) to the exact word used by the patient in his self-report of the case. While wishing to see another person naked, the patient feared that others knew his intimate thoughts or that the thoughts themselves would bring about a real disaster in the world: "in wishing this, I had *an uncanny feeling, as though something must happen if I thought such things, and as though I must do all sorts of things to prevent it*" (SE 10: 162). He feared, in other words, that someone else had broken into his psychic interiority (the most intimate dwelling in oneself or with oneself) unbeknownst to him.

Whatever the uncanny feeling is obsessed with, it is always obsessed with home—that is, with not being at home in one's own home, be it the psyche or the world. The obsession of Freud's patient has to do with the possibility that the people closest to him know his thoughts without him communicating them to anyone. He experiences a threat to the integrity of his inner psychic life, breached, broken into by others without his consent or control. His obsession is reignited in situations when thoughts are deemed immodest or impure: it is as though they would break out of their mental dwelling place and spill over into outside reality, wreaking havoc in it. This spillage and this being inhabited by others are, of course, the hallmarks of an ecological subject—including the Freudian ego—albeit in a less literal key.

When Freud turns his attention to "*the* uncanny," *das Unheimlich*, in 1919, he begins by noting that it is "related to what is frightening—to what arouses dread and horror" (SE 17: 219). The patient, whose case he had described ten years prior, was not horrified, in the first instance, by an external event but by the collapse of the boundaries between the inner and the outer, by his conviction that he could not keep his thoughts secret and that the most impious among these could trigger deaths and the like in the world. The "dread and horror" of the uncanny are the horror and dread of losing the *ideal* of one's ecological and egological dwelling as a sealed container, impermeable and secure, heavily guarded and administered in a sovereign fashion. Horrified, one is still at home, if no longer capable of safeguarding this untenable ideal, from the perspective of which anything short of absolute mastery and control over admission and sojourn is expulsion and homelessness. For its part, psychoanalysis also plays the role of the uncanny with respect to the ego/

eco-subject, who—we've heard Freud contend—is "*not master in its own house*" (SE 18: 143).

Freud adds that "the uncanny is that class of the frightening which leads back to what is known of old and long familiar" (SE 17: 220). And what is more thoroughly "known of old" and more familiar to us than our homes, where we know our way unthinkingly, intuitively, thanks to a habituation that transforms our dwellings into our second skin? When, in the course of his investigation, Freud consults foreign dictionaries and "other languages" to hone the sense of the uncanny (on another occasion, it would be propitious to a more complete unfolding of the argument to think through the question of uncanniness in language—not only one's mother tongue or a "foreign" language one speaks and understands, uncannily residing in it, but also of language broadly understood as modes of communication, expression, and being outside the human sphere, particularly with respect to the inhabitation of the human by these languages and their own uncanniness in the world of environmental devastation), the English entry gives a clue, which the psychoanalyst does not readily notice. Besides *uncanny*, this entry includes the following senses: *uncomfortable, uneasy, gloomy, dismal, ghastly; (of a house) haunted; (of a man) a repulsive fellow* (SE 17: 221). A haunted house comes close to the *Unheimlich*, the unhomely home, strange and familiar at the same time, because it is inhabited by ghosts. A dwelling contains more inhabitants than one suspects. The psychic dwelling is haunted by the unconscious; the ecological dwelling is haunted by everything and everyone threatening to make it uninhabitable (above or below all, the byproducts of the dump, the techno-unconscious that swells on a planetary scale); the textual dwelling is haunted by all the other authors, named and unnamed, whose work, words, and thoughts are interlaced with its threads—and now by AI.

The feeling that there is more going on than is evident, even and especially in the intimacy of different dwellings, is the kernel of the uncanny. A haunting is a doubling: apparently living alone, an inhabitant of a haunted dwelling is more than one, doubled by the ghost. The uncanny is the intrusion—more often than not only vaguely discernible, its fine-grained details obscure—of the double that one is to oneself into everyday life, which is why "this uncanny is in reality nothing new or alien, but something which is familiar and old-established in the mind and which has become alienated from it only through the process of repression." "This reference to the factor of repression," Freud continues, "enables us, furthermore, to understand Schelling's definition of the uncanny as something which ought to have remained hidden but has come to light" (SE 17: 241).

The uncanny is a dark mirror placed before us, in which we see—albeit still vaguely, or enigmatically as St. Paul would say—a part of ourselves that is not a part of our conscious self-perception: we see the other within. The uncanny of an ecological dwelling is, likewise, its own underside, which is usually imperceptible: the dormant volcanic forces that may suddenly come to the fore, the rivers whose basins may flood, microplastics embedded in organismic tissues and in every place on the planet . . . Alienated and repressed, these tend to remain hidden but, for one or another reason, come to light, disrupting ecosystems and organisms, while remaining largely unprocessable on strictly conscious grounds. Rather than allegories for the unconscious in the human psyche, they are aspects of the ecological unconscious that mold the ecological dwelling as much as destabilize and defamiliarize it: mold by destabilizing it.

The fact that, when it comes to the ecosystemic or planetary dwelling, the repressed that is momentarily uncovered there goes under the contested name "the Anthropocene" is a symptom of uncanniness. However limited the gender, race, class, and geographical belonging and situatedness of the main culprits behind the Anthropocene may be, the name of the human (Greek *anthropos*, which comes to denominate this geological era and which has already cropped up in these pages) functions precisely as the *double* of the human. It is our repressed double, who comes to supplant our divine double[1] and who consists of the unwasting waste, the immortal, non-decomposable remains of the techno-body that haunts humankind and the entire planet, in keeping with the dynamics of the uncanny. And it transgresses not only the boundaries between the inside and the outside (of a body, of the species, etc.) but also distinctions between kinds of dwelling (psychic, bodily, ecological, planetary) when its byproducts get lodged everywhere.

At this point, we arrive at a surprising intermediate conclusion: the wound to human narcissism that is the ecological crisis—the fourth wound, to be added to the other three Freud lists—reinforces this same narcissism. If the *anthropos* of the Anthropocene is the double of humanity, then this double is both a blow to and a cure for human narcissism: it ushers in death on the mass scale of species' extinction (potentially not sparing *Homo sapiens*) and at the same time promises a near immortality to the human, by preserving its geological traces and their long-lingering effects.

The complication of accelerated death and immortality in the figure of the double does not escape Freud's attention. Relying on the work Otto Rank developed on the theme of the double, Freud agrees that "the 'double' was originally an insurance against the destruction of the ego" and treats "this invention of doubling as a preservation against extinction," driven by narcissism. "But when this stage [of primary narcissism, MM] has been surmounted," he writes, "the 'double' reverses its aspect. From having been an assurance of immortality, it becomes the uncanny harbinger of death" (SE 17: 235). The reversion of the aspect of the double that is *anthropos*, or the human of the Anthropocene, is happening on a planetary scale, a reversion that, at the sociopolitical level, implies the death of Man (the ideological persona of a white, male, Western, heteronormative, middle-to-upper-class subject—and his accomplices perhaps not fitting these rigid identity categories) whose thinking, values, and practices had culminated in a worldwide ecological catastrophe. It is this persona or personage, as much ideological as it is historical, that is now uncannily revaluated as the harbinger of death and that is putting up tremendous resistance in the shape of extreme-right nationalism, climate change denial, and urgent appeals to colonize space and other planets.

In the Freudian scheme, reversion signals that the stage of primary narcissism is being surmounted, or that it has been already surmounted. In the case of the Anthropocene, however, it is not clear whether primary narcissism is overcome or actually strengthened, redoubling not only humankind with its techno-body and its waste but also insinuating the persistent (ghostly) presence of anthropogenic artifacts into virtually all ecosystems. What is uncanny is their merging with the planet, the becoming-geological of *anthropos*, or of its double, as a "harbinger of death," as much as their recall of an immemorial past, which had hitherto remained hidden and has now become uncovered. Disavowing this double, pretending that it does not exist, proponents of fusion with mother nature stubbornly cling to primary narcissism, purified and rarefied, that is to say fabricated from the standpoint of its inexorable overcoming and shorn of any overtones of the uncanny: coming back home to this squeaky clean to the point of sterility earthly home is leaving the earth as it is, as a geo-dump. It follows then that one of the most consequential differences between the doom of the Anthropocene and the naïve optimism beaming from the worshippers of mother nature is the presence or absence of the uncanny effect, disclosing what was hidden and allowing one to grow toward and mature in relation to one's own double.

Freud is aware that, touching upon the uncanny, he brings to light a vital dimension of psychoanalysis itself, which busies itself with unearthing deeply buried unconscious materials. "Indeed, I should not be surprised," he writes, "to hear that psychoanalysis, which is concerned with laying bare these hidden forces, has itself become uncanny to many people for that very reason" (SE 17: 243). In other words, psychoanalysis, with its conclusions and the practices substantiating them, is the meta-uncanny, an estranging thing, de-familiarizing the self-conception of the human in touch with the untamed and untamable, animal, vegetal, geological, planetary forces that have always inhabited the human under the sign of severe repression. The psychoanalytic meta-uncanny is, therefore, as much psychological (more precisely, psycho-physiological) as it is ecological: the human is inhabited by its in- or non-human double, while also inhabiting this double, estranged to the *n*th degree and intimately familiar at the same time.

By interrelating the comfortingly familiar and the utterly unfamiliar, the known and the strange, the uncanny performs the work of integration that aims beyond primary narcissism *and* its mere reversion. But it does not, by any means, amount to the New Age ideal of becoming whole; the unconscious and its "hidden forces" can never be digested either as such or in each of their parts; the shock of unfamiliarity (above all, with oneself) does not wear off after a while. Often, the uncanny assumes the form of "dismembered limbs, a severed head, a hand cut off at the wrist, as in a fairy tale of Hauff's, feet which dance by themselves" (SE 17: 244), so that integration proceeds by way of disintegration, by highlighting the overzealous analytical drive, which is one of the faces of Thanatos (here, psychoanalysis is uncanny in an additional sense, not intended by Freud when he ascribes uncanniness to its operations; it would perhaps be better to call it "soul-work," *psychoergia*, or *psychoergy*, seeing that "work" combines analytic and synthetic activities). Isn't this what scientific reductivism ultimately looks like? Not content with chopping the body up into parts in order to know the bits and pieces of the corpse this body will have been, it analyzes organs and tissues further and dissolves them in biochemical processes, electric signaling, genetic makeup, etc.—all in a sweeping centuries-old tendency of cutting knowledge off from life, of de-eroticizing it, of subjugating knowledge and its "production" to the death drive.

Although Freud does not quite put it in these terms, the uncanny involves a double movement (note that the *dynamic form* of the uncanny is also double, as is its *content*). On the one hand, the uncanny gives a sense of the deadening of the living—as we've seen in the case of the crude or refined reductivism, rampant analysis, amputations, castration anxiety, phantasies of being buried alive, etc. On the other hand, it has to do with the exact opposite, namely with the enlivening of the dead—wooden crocodiles who come alive in a haunted house, or, both closer to and further away from us, the long-dead plant and animal matter forced to be born again from the body of the earth, set ablaze, and made to yield energy before quickly dying a second time and leaving planet-wide traces of death and destruction in its wake.

The ecological sense of the uncanny thus comes up against its limits. In a Hegelian key, Freud returns to the speculative identity of the uncanny and the intimately familiar, of the homely and the unhomely, toward the end of his essay, noting that "the *unheimlich* is what was once *heimisch*, familiar; the prefix '*un*' ['un-'] is the token of repression" (SE 17: 245). The question is, nonetheless: Are all unconscious materials equally worth unearthing? Is it even possible to uncover some among them? Isn't there a hiddenness that is crucial to the flourishing of life, as with roots buried in the soil that, when exposed, no longer sustain the rest of the plant? Aren't fossil layers more than the reserves contained in the bowels of the earth? Aren't they the integral parts of this earth, which also assure the relative stability of its upper layers? Aren't the non-transparency of the skin and the invisibility of the microbial flora on its surfaces and other bodily membranes necessary for a basic relation to one's own body and to the bodies of others? And isn't repression at times indistinguishable from the life-giving obscurity which Heraclitus associated with the favorite activity of nature itself, notably its love (*philia*, with strong erotic undercurrents) of self-encryption, hiding?

V

Vultures, kites, and other ani-things

It's October 7, 2024. I am observing four vultures as they are circling above one of many open-air dumps in Terra dei fuochi, just beneath the steep slopes of Mount Vesuvius. They are gliding on airflows, occasionally dropping or rising apparently not of their own volition, and in this they are nearly indistinguishable from the gigantic pieces of black plastic lining the ground and occasionally carried up with the wind. The vultures and plastic are the ani-things (animal or animated things) no longer conforming to the logic of fetishism as Freud develops it. They are also the any-things, existing under the sign of non-differentiation in the age of the dump, in which unconscious agglomeration and non-decomposability predominate.

The scene in the vicinity of the Vesuvius unfolded before my eyes three days after reading Freud's analysis of Leonardo da Vinci's childhood memory, which had apparently also involved a vulture. Contemplating the flight of vultures, Leonardo notes: "It seems that I was always destined to be so deeply concerned with vultures; for I recall as one of my very earliest memories that while I was in my cradle a vulture came down to me, and opened by mouth with its tail, and struck me many times with its tail against my lips" (SE 11: 82). Freud relies on his words in the German translation by Marie Herzfeld, which, as the editor James Strachey observes, contains two "inaccuracies": "'*nibio*' [*nibbio* in modern Italian] should be 'kite' not 'vulture', and '*dentro*', 'within', is omitted" (SE 11: 82, FN1). Once the inaccuracies are corrected, it turns out that, in Leonardo's memory, the tail of a kite both struck his lips and pushed past them inside his mouth.

The associative chain vulture-kite is evidently at work in Leonardo's own account, because it is in the course of describing the flight of vultures that the memory of the kite turns up. If the object that presumably struck the infant Leonardo on his lips and went into his mouth was an inanimate one (the tail of a kite) rather than an organ of a living being (a bird), that is because there is an unconscious demand for an extra line of repressive defense in order to divert attention from the person who could have been behind these actions—in Freud's interpretation, the mother who either planted passionate kisses on the infant's lips, or suckled him, or indeed both (SE 11: 87ff.). Whatever the reason behind the confusion, for the unconscious, there is no significant difference between a bird and an ingenious flying contraption, especially seeing that the wind is an animating, life-giving force, as Freud emphasizes with regard to the mythologies of the vulture and its (or her) reproduction. The non-differentiation between them from the vantage point of the unconscious lends itself felicitously to the arsenal of psychological defenses, allied with the conscious ego.

The vulture-kite, then, is Leonardo's mother—an ani-thing that gives him life from the position of possible lifelessness and that loves him, literally, to death. All this is still in need of unpacking; in the meantime, let's begin with the basics.

The vulture is a rare female specimen in Freud's psychoanalytic bestiary. Reflections about the mother as a vulture lead Freud back to ancient Egypt, where "the mother is represented by a picture of a vulture. The Egyptians also worshipped a mother goddess, who was represented as having a vulture's head," he adds (SE 11: 88). Moreover, a vulture is female without a male: "We learn from these sources [Horapollo's *Hieroglyphica*, as well as Strabo, Plutarch, and Ammianus Marcellinus, MM] that the vulture was regarded as a symbol of motherhood because only female vultures were believed to exist; there were, it was thought, no males of the species" (SE 11: 88). In this, the vulture is akin to a phoenix, who, while not exclusively female, is one of a kind and, therefore, does not need a mate of the other sex in order to reproduce. But she is also glaringly different from the phoenix, who is an inheritor of phallic Egyptian solar deities. Combined with the breakdown of the Oedipus complex, which simply does not work in the case of Leonardo ("he had had a mother, but no father"; "the fact of Leonardo's illegitimate birth is in harmony with his vulture phantasy" [SE 11: 90; 91], plus the idea is that Leonardo had two mothers: the birth mother and the one who adopted him, or a mother and a grandmother, as depicted in "The Virgin and Child with Saint Anne"), this feature suggests another hypothesis about the mother goddess than the one formed in the context of geo-psycho-analysis.

As a mother goddess, in line with the pre- or non-Indo-European great goddesses, such as the Basque Mari or the Aztec Tlaltecuhtli, the vulture combines light and darkness, the sky and the earth, life and death. Soaring high in the sky, she drops down to feed on carrion, on the rotting flesh that will receive a new lease of life in her, as her. She is a point of indistinction between the extremes that are set apart in patriarchal modes of thinking and imagination, not least among these Eros and Thanatos, as well as an inanimate thing and an animated being. She is, in other words, a singular figuration of the immanent earth, who is the earth and the sky and oceanic waters and volcanic fire—the Anything or Ani-thing of vitality and mortality.

To be sure, conflations of sexes and species ensue, according to Freud's reading of the Leonardo case: the bird's tail (*coda*) "is one of the most familiar symbols and substitutive expressions for the male organ" (SE 11: 85); "the child becomes familiar with the cow's udder whose function is that of a nipple, but whose shape and position under the belly make it resemble a penis" (SE 11: 87); and, finally, the mother is identified with the father, resulting in "a homosexual situation" (SE 11: 93). So, Freud opts for the interpretation of Leonardo's phantasy and life by teasing out from it a homosexual "inversion," rather than a reclaiming of original bisexuality (the mix of masculine and feminine features on "the strangely beautiful face of the Florentine Mona Lisa del Giocondo" [SE 11: 107] should have given him an appropriate clue) or even of a polysexuality, of a piece with polymorphous perversity, edging still further toward the realm of animate beings and inanimate objects passing into and for one another.

Just as we have gone back to the "basics," we have spotted a limit of Freud's analysis: he interprets the incarnation of a mother goddess from a patriarchal point of view—that is, under the sway of the Oedipus complex and within the *philosophical* framework of patriarchy, where the life instinct and the death drive, for instance, are organized in relations of mutual opposition. Freud intuits the shared ground of the two in their capacity to quell libidinal tensions either temporarily or permanently, but he still holds onto their antithetical nature. That is probably why crucial aspects of Leonardo's phantasy escape his analytical scrutiny, details that, when brought to light, change the texture of the case and give it an ecological twist.

The association between this case and ecology does not pivot exclusively on the vulture at the heart of Leonardo's phantasy being an animal, or, better, it has to do with the *kind* of animal she is and with the *organs* of the vulture that come into contact with the lips and mouth of the infant Leonardo. Freud oscillates between the image of the vulture's tail as the mother's lips, her nipple, and a penis, but he forgets the obvious, namely that its place on the bird's body is closest to the anus, the organ of excretion. The oral and the anal phases collapse into one another along with the distinction between Eros and Thanatos. The nourishing mother—life-giving with the milk of her breast, with the kisses of maternal love, and with the phallus attributed to her—is dispensing not only whip-like strikes on the infant's lips but also her waste, feeding her beloved son with it. And, as a vulture, she, too, feeds on waste, on carrion, the rotting animal bodies that mirror and amplify the excremental gift she offers. The circularity of the anus-to-mouth scene, which Freud reconstructs based on the German translation of Leonardo's vision, is that of ecology without its idealizing white- or green-washing: all nourishment is nourishment on death and toward death, drawn from the earth, in which the dead are rotting, no matter how high in the air the figure of the earth soars in the shape of a vulture and no matter, too, how plants are nourished by the sun in the glorious ideality of another mode of energy generation. Ecology as divine coprophagy, then.

The gravitas of this image is diluted with the kite tail fluttering in the wind, according to the exact word *nibio* that appears in Leonardo's diaries. A useless but entertaining toy is of a piece with the nourishing and threatening bird, who embodies all of nature. This, too, is ecology—the ecology of ani-thing. The wind is the force of animation, when it comes both to a kite and to a vulture: the former depends on its flows for movement, whereas the latter reproduces thanks to it, according to the belief system prevalent in ancient Egypt: "How then were vultures supposed to be impregnated if all of them were female? This is a point fully explained in a passage in Horapollo. At a certain time, these birds pause in mid-flight, open their vagina and are impregnated by the wind" (SE 11: 89).

Two points are of note here. First, fertility and, by implication, sexuality are dispersed in the entire biosphere among organisms and the elements (including the wind, the moving air masses, which are also responsible for the sexual reproduction of plants and other organisms who spread spores, and not only pollen or seeds). Second, the moment of impregnation entails a "pause in mid-flight," in the course of which a living bird becomes, for all intents and purposes, indistinguishable from a kite. The renewal of life in an offspring is possible thanks to a symbolic or not-so-symbolic death, the vulture merging with the figure of an ani-thing, hovering at the mercy of the wind, somewhat like a large plastic bag.

Another layer of material that escapes Freud's analytical attention has to do with himself, with his own projection onto the material at hand. Commenting on the name of the Egyptian mother goddess, represented by a vulture, he asks, rhetorically: "This goddess's name was pronounced *Mut*. Can the similarity to the sound of our word *Mutter* ['mother'] be merely a coincidence?" (SE 11: 88). "Our word" for *mother* is not, however, Leonardo's in Italian; it is, rather, Freud's identification with the son of *Mut* that comes to the fore. Similarly, the German association of the bird with a phallus would have been more revealing with regard to Freud than Leonardo: "the commonest expression in German for male sexual activity is *vögeln* ['to bird': *Vogel* is the German for 'bird']" adds something else to the "small fragments from a whole mass of connected ideas" (SE 11: 125), something that is peculiar to Freud. Finally, Leonardo's nearly obsessive interest in and investigations of "the problem of the flight of birds" are said to be "derived from the sexual researches of his childhood" (SE 11: 92). But what about Freud's own detailed, nearly obsessive interest in Leonardo, resulting in a book-length study of his "case"? Is it due to a second-degree fascination with (technically speaking, identification and projection, or projective identification) the same issues Freud diagnoses in his subject?

Freud's blind spots and, in particular, his incapacity to think the vulture-kite-goddess-mother outside the frame of the Oedipus complex undermine his comprehension of the Leonardo case as much as of the immanent ecological paradigm that subtends the transcendent nature of patriarchal cults and modes of thinking. For instance, Freud writes that "in dreams the wish to be able to fly is to be understood as nothing else than a longing to be capable of sexual performance. This is an early infantile wish" (SE 11: 126). And he observes that "the great Leonardo remained like a child for the whole of his life in more than one way" (SE 11: 127). In Leonardo's phantasy, it is the vulture who takes flight, which implies, for Freud, that the infant Leonardo is prepared to assume a passive position in the sexual relation. Nonetheless, "an early infantile wish" belongs within the matrix of polymorphous perversity: the sexualization of the entire body and its environs; play unconnected to the pressure of "performing"; a capacity and a sensibility irreducible to pure activity. "Remaining like a child" for the whole of one's life is refusing to give up on polymorphously perverse, ecological desire.

The vulture soars and circles above, then suddenly drops down. All four of them do so over the dump in Terra dei fuochi. Besides this vertical dimension, a subtler horizontal one: the circulation of life and death, nourishment, desire, excrements, decomposition, reassembly. The lips and the mouth are the organs where these movements are registered, at a certain pace, at the rhythm of the vulture's tail dispensing pleasure and pain, waste and desire, the cradle and the grave merging into one. Leonardo feels, more sharply than anyone, these elemental kisses that are not without their violence, their inversions and perversions (tail to face; vulture to kite; inside out). He receives the imprints of ani-thing and then sends them on, along the multiple trajectories of his art and science.

An appropriate postscript to this chapter is a story from January 2024, when two activists from the Riposte Alimentaire (Food Counterattack) movement threw pumpkin soup onto the glass-protected Mona Lisa painting at the Louvre.[1] The sad irony of this action comes to light thanks to the phantasy of the vulture and her tail attack on Leonardo's lips, sublimated into Mona Lisa's mysterious smile. Isn't the vulture's diet the most "sustainable food"—a key demand of Riposte Alimentaire—imaginable: feeding off the dead, letting them live otherwise, as nourishment, not just in the entrails of the earth but in the birds' stomachs and intestines? More than five hundred years after Leonardo had made his diary entry about a large bird of prey hitting his infant lips with her tail, Mona Lisa's lips were hit by splashes of canned pumpkin soup. One can only receive this piece of belated news with a vulture smile.

W

Wish fulfillment and green dreams

It is well known that psychoanalysis deals primarily with substitutes: the substitutes of paternal and maternal figures, of bodily organs (or even the entire body) and things in fetishism, and, importantly, of ways of satisfying desire. When satisfaction cannot be obtained directly from the love object, libidinal energy is cathected to something or someone else standing for it. Symptoms, including of the neurotic and obsessive kind, are substitute satisfactions and knots of cathexes, as are hallucinations and dreams.

One can write an entire treatise on the role of wish fulfillment in the ecological crisis with the intricate symptomatology, hallucinated states of reality, substitute cathexes, and dreams, vacillating between utopian visions and apocalyptic nightmares. I will limit myself here to a consideration of wish fulfillment in "green dreams."

While the lack of a significant, concerted response to the global environmental emergency has been often compared to a failure to wake up to the severity of the situation, ours is not a dreamless sleep. Ecological dreams range from representations of ecology as a space of autochthony to the purity of belonging, harmony, and peace. These dreams also consider ecology to be the key to solving all other economic, racial, gender troubles and to putting an end to the nightmares of the end of the world. As Freud writes in his 1932 revision of dream-theory, included in his *New Introductory Lectures to Psychoanalysis*, however, "in every dream an instinctual wish has to be represented as fulfilled" (SE 22: 18–19). Wish fulfillment in dreams yields substitute satisfaction, starting with "the wish to sleep and intentional turning away from the external world" (SE 22: 19). It is a fulfillment that, in its very process and its presuppositions, is separate from the external world—that is, from the actual ecological state of affairs. But what, exactly, is the otherwise forbidden wish that is fulfilled in ecological dreams *only* through substitute satisfaction?

Starting with the positive dimension of ecological dreams, the indication is that the "repudiated thought" (SE 22: 18) at the core of ecology is so disturbing that it is substituted not just with an image but with a color: green. A green transition, green energy, green economy, the Green New Deal, and many other terms to boot rely on the abstraction of color, loosely alluding to chlorophyl, to represent the instinctual wish animating them as fulfilled. These are, of course, the concepts spawned by the hegemonic ideology that is displacing subversive desires and their expression in ideas onto a neutral (politically and psychically neutralized) background. The color green functions in ideological discourse analogously to a green screen in cinema that allows filmmakers to insert any image into a scene by replacing the screen's color hues. More than a displaced, condensed, distorted dream image, greenness is a neutralizing substratum for any such image that may emerge in an ecological dream.

Succinctly put, substitute fulfillment is called for because the wish cannot be accommodated on the grounds of global capital. "Use value" and "externalities," to which ecology is relegated from the standpoint of capital itself, do not have a chance to be on the centerstage of systemic concerns unless they are translated into exchange values, monetized, capitalized, commodified, and rendered "internal" to the logic of capital, which is indifferent to their destruction, be it productive or non-productive. Yet, the desire for a livable world is so basic that, presupposed by the life instinct itself, Freud does even mention it. The minimal satisfaction of *this* desire is a precondition for the satisfaction of *any* desire, which is why it cannot be left on the sidelines, receiving instead a substitute, dream satisfaction in the ecological discourse itself.

The negative dimension of ecological dreams is also tied to wish fulfillment. For instance, taking the view that the ever more frequent and extreme "natural disasters" are the punishment meted out by harsh mother nature corresponds to a wish of something or someone within ourselves bent on sadistically punishing us. Desiring the extinction of humankind belongs to the most radical manifestation of this phenomenon. Freud weighs in on the general logic behind this as follows: "Punishment-dreams, too, are fulfilments of wishes, though not of wishes of the instinctual impulses but of those of the critical, censoring and punishing agency in the mind" (SE 22: 27). Despite generating further anxiety, a traumatic dream, as well, is "an *attempt* at the fulfilment of a wish" (SE 22: 29), notably one of undoing the unconscious fixation of trauma, of getting unstuck, of working through it, of "moving on," rather than constantly rotating in its orbit. This is not to deny the severity of the actual crisis, which would be somehow exaggerated in nightmarish dreams; all I am suggesting is that the *interpretative relation* of these dreams to the crisis is that of wish fulfillment by the sadistic superego.

In his much earlier, original approach to dream-work in *The Interpretation of Dreams*, Freud tackles a similar dilemma when faced with the "dream of the burning child." The father of a recently deceased child falls asleep while an old man keeps watch of the body, "with tall candles standing round it." "After a few hours' sleep, the father had a dream that *his child was standing beside his bed, caught him by the arm and whispered to him reproachfully: 'Father, don't you see I am burning?'*" (SE 5: 509). Waking up, the father sees a glare from the other room where the child's body is laid out, rushes in, and discovers "that the old watchman had dropped off to sleep and that the wrappings and one of the arms of his beloved child's dead body had been burned by a lighted candle that had fallen on them" (SE 5: 509).

Freud does not advance the hypothesis that the father wished for the child's body to burn and this wish's anxiety-producing fulfillment in a dream coincided with an event in the world. Perhaps, Freud himself recoils from such a hypothesis for reasons of projection or quasi-transference, but he does hint at it at the head of the section on wish fulfillment in his dream book. "The dream of the burning child at the beginning of this chapter," he writes, "gives us a welcome opportunity of considering the difficulties with which the theory of wish-fulfilment is faced" (SE 5: 550).

Interpreting the dream of the burning child, Freud leaves suspended the question of "what part was played in this [dream, MM] by wish fulfilment" and instead approvingly cites Aristotle's definition of a dream in terms of "thinking that persists [...] in the state of sleep." Wishing becomes but one of many instances of thinking, which includes judgments, inferences, expectations, intentions, and so forth. But this maneuver contravenes the logic of psychoanalysis, according to which thinking, including its apparently abstract varieties, is rooted in affect, in quanta of raw libidinal energy. The disturbing possibility of wish fulfillment *must* be contemplated, in combination with the lapses of judgment that result in surrounding the laid-out body with candles and appointing an elderly person to invigilate over it.

Is the nightmare of the ecological "house on fire" not similar in its structure to the "dream of the burning child"? The dream of a planet that whispers to us reproachfully, "Don't you see I am burning?" coincides with the body of the earth that is really burning, roasting in the flames of global heating, themselves the reflections of centuries-long combustion of the earth's fossil contents. The horror at the thought and the feel of a burning planet is mingled with wish fulfillment, the unconscious desire to see it burn. Simultaneously wishing and not wishing for something to happen generates psychic tension stronger than disavowal, which, as the acknowledgment and repudiation of a piece of reality, is comparable to cognitive dissonance, with cathexes already diminished, dimmed down to the intensities of a more or less abstract thinking. Waking up from the dream does not nullify its complex, self-contradictory libidinal structure. The ecological discourse of "a house on fire" is, therefore, not as unequivocal as it may appear.

The hypothesis regarding the self-undermining and self-affirming character of wish fulfillment in dreams is supported by Freud's reflections on distortion, which is attributable to the censoring faculty and the impediments it sets up on the path of a straightforward manifestation of desire. In a short 1932 text, Freud contends that "the dream (or the distortion which characterizes it) is the expression of a compromise, the evidence of a conflict between the mutually incompatible impulses and strivings of our mental life. And let us not forget that the same process, the same interplay of forces, which explains the dreams of a normal sleeper, gives us the key to understanding all the phenomena of neurosis and psychosis" (SE 22: 222).

The "conflict between the mutually incompatible impulses and strivings of our mental life" not only precedes and permeates wish fulfillment through and through; it also cuts through its outcome, the actualization implied in *fulfillment*. Negative affect ranging from light unhappiness to a severe depression that may afflict someone whose wish is *actually* fulfilled is far from accidental: it is a sign of the quelling of desire, however temporary, and, as such, the premonition and interjection of the death drive, in which the tension of desire is quelled permanently, rather than temporarily. Every wish fulfillment is, to a certain extent, suicidal—and suicidal wishes, such as those for the planet to burn, reveal the hidden truth of wish fulfillment in general, notably the obscure co-belonging of life instincts and the death drive, underlying occasional strategic compromises between incompatible mental strivings. The dark side of wish fulfillment should not be easily dismissed, least of all in the case of "green dreams" and planetary nightmares.

Although Freud contends that the "dreams of a normal sleeper give us the key to understanding all the phenomena of neurosis and psychosis," the dice are loaded in favor of the latter condition. Dreams should be placed, Freud argues, "in a class along with other psychopathological formations" and be "revealed [. . .], as it were, as the normal psychoses of human beings" (SE 22: 221). "Normal psychoses" are both non-pathological and indispensable to everyday psycho-social functioning: a dose of psychosis with its distorted wish fulfillments during one's sleep is a prerequisite for non-psychotic behavior in waking life. But what if one doesn't quite wake up from green dreams and nightmares? Then, in a lasting, ideologically induced sleep, psychosis is constant and highly pathological.

In dreams and in a schizophrenic state, Freud sees "hallucinatory wishful psychoses" (SE 14: 230) that flourish under the auspices of regression (SE 14: 229). Simply put, one hallucinates the satisfaction that is denied to one in reality. Freud does not operate with a naïve distinction between reality and phantasy here: a hallucinated dream-wish "meets with belief in the reality of its fulfilment" (SE 14: 229) and "hallucination brings belief in reality with it" (SE 14: 230). This positive feedback loop allows hallucination to keep itself intact *as if* it were real—until, that is, an actual stressor from the outside world or from the hallucinating subject's own physiology cuts through the webs of belief in the truth of dreamt-up wish fulfillment.

The denialist camp clings onto the hallucination that the climate is stable, that catastrophic climate change is not happening. The wish for stability, for the preservation of the status quo, prevails at all costs, carrying in its hallucinatory structure a belief in the reality of its fulfillment. In another key, the dreams of eco-activists are not infrequently hallucinated wishes, saddled with belief in their reality. Relinquishing oil and replacing it with battery-powered cars, for instance, does not do away with the logic and the economy of extractivism (here, of lithium) nor does it solve the problem of recycling spent-up batteries. The polemics around climate change assume the form of a phantasmagoric battle of hallucinations, of wishful not-thinking.

X

Xylophone magic: echoes and eco's

I have long argued for an auditory, rather than a visual or a purely conceptual, appreciation of ecology. In *Green Mass* (2021), Swedish composer Peter Schuback and I tried to listen philosophically and musically to the proposals of St. Hildegard of Bingen as they speak or sing to us, to listen, above all, to *how* she would have or could have listened to creation as *symphonia*, discerning the singular resonances of each soul with its body and the co-sounding of soul-bodies with their others.

Freud himself was no fan of music. In fact, as Ernest Jones reminisces, "Freud's aversion to music was one of his well-known characteristics. One well remembers the pained expression on his face on entering a restaurant or beer garden where there was a band and how quickly his hands would go over his ears to drown the sound."[1] The openness (indeed, the open*ed*ness) of the ear to sound that an infant cannot block out, as Derrida reminds us, echoing Freud,[2] has perhaps something to do with it—the adult taking charge (primarily of himself via what he is willing and what he is unwilling to admit into himself, including at the auditory level) by contrast with the infant's traumatic helplessness. But this is not to deny that psychic ecologies are also sonorous: doesn't Freud's early abandonment of attempts to cure through hypnosis in favor of the talking cure provide the most vociferous evidence to this effect?

With regard to sounds and the tentative bridge between their echoes and an ecologically inflected psychoanalysis, I want to focus on a certain machine, an instrument of the musical kind. I will transpose the analogy Freud makes between the conscious-unconscious mind, memory and forgetting, line tracings, etc. and another machine, "the mystic writing-pad," onto a xylophone, which is itself a "transposing instrument," producing either higher or lower pitches than those indicated in the music written for them. Here, pitches are relative, rather than exact! Their transposition, problematizing the notion of translation as an accurate transfer from one language to another, is the model for and the modulation of the relation between consciousness and the unconscious, between the conscious-unconscious psyche and the world.

A xylophone, pre-dated and known across Africa and Asia by other names (*dimbila, gyil, mbaire, silimba, balenjeh, ranat*, or *gambang*, to mention but a few), literally means "the voice of wood," or "the sound of wood." It is the voice of the otherwise voiceless, rendering anything like an exact translation—be it linguistic, conceptual, or sonorous—meaningless. While itself voiceless, xylem (the vascular tissue of plants, which, like the xylophone, retains in its name one of the Greek words for wood, *xylon*) is crisscrossed by communication channels: it transports water, as well as nutrients, from the roots upward. To let xylem resound is to bring to the auditory register its silent intermediacy, to become a middle for the middle, an echo of the eco, which is the place of the ego.

And isn't that how a conscious "translation" of unconscious desire works, never giving the subject access to desire *itself, as such*, but always betraying it, expressing it through what it is not? Freud's poignant reflections on negation attain here their deeper sense: the stirrings of the unconscious twist into their opposite at the conscious level of expression not only due to the forces of repression, but also, and especially, due to their givenness to consciousness in no other form than as what they are *not*. Rather than a failure, which it would be in a paradigm guided by the value of exactitude, such twisting is the very possibility of conscious expression. At any rate, that which or the one who speaks through a xylophone is matter itself, wood (rosewood, among many other kinds) and the woods, living and dead, or dead and enlivened by the equally dead mallets striking the wooden bars. Uncanny. The first precursory indication crops up as a result: life and death instincts infinitely echo one another.

In the analogy between the mystic writing-pad and its double inscriptions, on the one hand, and conscious and unconscious traces, on the other, Freud attends to the different materials constituting the upper and the lower layers of the device: "The Mystic Pad is a slab of dark brown resin or wax with paper edging; over the slab is laid a thin transparent sheet, the top end of which is firmly secured to the slab while its bottom end rests on it [. . .] This transparent sheet is the more interesting part of the little device. It itself consists of two layers, which can be detached from each other except at their two ends. The upper layer is a transparent piece of celluloid; the lower layer is made of thin translucent waxed paper" (SE 19: 228–9). The doubling is itself doubled: one always becomes two and the surface reveals its own depth, which, in turn, has a surface and a depth. Although none of the materials Freud describes are wooden, these, too, are the qualities of matter and its relation to form: depth and surface, the constitution and the look (*eidos*) of things, the lower layer splitting into upper and lower, matter (including psychic matter) coming replete with its singularly befitting forms. At the extreme, the relativity and infinite regress in the relation of surface and depth suggest that there is no pure unconscious—unformed, untraced, undelimited, and hence timeless.

A xylophone plays with the upper and the lower, which itself becomes the upper vis-à-vis another layer, in the registers of matter and sound. The wooden bars that are struck by mallets are the lower surfaces, each of them tuned to the pitch of a musical scale, albeit at relative pitches, related to but not coinciding with the pitches for which xylophone music is written (transposition). Still below the bars, concert xylophones have tube resonators to enhance the tone. The lower level is the upper in relation to another one.

So, who or what sounds when a xylophonist plays a xylophone? The mallet or the bars? Their consonance? This consonance as it is amplified by the resonators? The music that has been composed or the music that is played at another pitch thanks to transposition? Similarly, who or what speaks in a therapeutic setting and in everyday life? The conscious subject or the unconscious? The consciousness *of* the unconscious? Their consonance or mutual silencing and partial amplification? The overtly intended or the deeply desired but sublimated or repressed? Symptoms are the "symphonetoms" of psychic life and death, form and matter, negotiating a difficult course between the fulfillment and the non-fulfillment of desire by resorting to the logic of substitution, of substitute satisfaction, which is of a piece with dis- or non-satisfaction. It is impossible to determine whether these *relata* are in tune or out of tune with one another without considering conjunctural factors and their modes of reception, for instance, when they become exceptionally disruptive to a person's daily life.

In the middle of it all is sound, which is always already sound*s*: vibrating in-between struck surfaces and their various resonances.[3] Sounds and their waves are ambient; they suffuse the atmosphere as much as the inner ear, while bouncing differently from material surfaces. Psychic matter, rather than materiality mimicking ideality even at the level of the word's "construction" with the suffix "-ality," is disclosed here as an interface between unconscious demands and the exteriority of the world that provides the tools for their—inevitably betrayed—expression. It is also the *wherein* of the sounding, the means and the medium among other variations on the middle. This psychic matter is the ego, which, as we've now heard after having silently read it, is *eco*. And, in our analogical scheme, it's not irrelevant what the matter of this matter actually is in a xylophone.

Among instruments that are closely related to a xylophone are a lithophone and a metallophone, where slabs of stone or metal produce different pitches when struck. We are dealing with wood, though. All kinds of matter have their memory, correlated to densities and dents, resistances and the ease of yielding, the longer or shorter timespans of the formative and de-formational processes they have undergone, and so forth. The memory of wood, however, adds something to this list of material memories, namely the histories of nourishment and, therefore, of life; energy flows that have traversed and constituted the tree; the synergies of solarity and decay, of the sun and the earth with water ... These are the "things" that resonate in every strike of the mallet on wooden bars of the xylophone, which is to say that the entire world co-sounds in, as, and with it. Likewise with the ego, resonating with the outside world and with desire as their in-between—not as a metallic, stony, or generally inorganic screen, but as psychic matter that is wooden and of the woods, rooted in the ancient *to threptikon*.

In the essay on the mystic writing-pad, Freud marvels at the holding together of permanence and impermanence, as far as the act or the fact of leaving traces is concerned, the erasure and the lingering on of impressions on sundry surfaces of the same contrivance, which "solves the problem of combining the two functions *by dividing them between two separate but interrelated component parts or systems*." "But this," he adds, "is precisely the way in which, according to the hypothesis which I mentioned just now, our mental apparatus performs its perceptual function" (SE 19: 230). For a psyche that is not entirely unconscious, time passes and doesn't pass, or, at least its passage is slowed down, letting the trace remain, while, in another part, everything passes so quickly that the passage itself doesn't as much as register. The life of the mind is this very division and interrelation of passing and non-passing, of a rhythm and its presumed absence.

The writing-pad is a support for visual marks that can lay a certain claim on permanence. There is no such thing in sound, the existence of sound-recording equipment notwithstanding. Sound is temporal through and through, from the silence or a sequence of prior sounds whence it emerges through to its sound*ing*, breaking into the sounds it has always been, and subsequent fizzling out or abrupt cessation and transition back to relative silence or to still other sounds. That said, the mystic writing-pad and the xylophone have something in common: both of them combine "two functions *by dividing them between two separate but interrelated component parts or systems*." Matter and memory are indistinguishable from one another in the body of the instrument, which is itself a sign and a repository of past life: organismic and elemental, ecosystemic and cosmic. This past life lives on, survives, and remembers what it has been as the wooden bars and mallets and resonators (or as wax and the stylus in the writing-pad). The sounding disperses and the sounded remains: together they form the infrastructure of sound tirelessly doubling in and against itself, of ecology, of the unconscious that splits into consciousness and the unconscious, of life and death, psychic and not only.

So, the ego is the first surface struck by the impressions from external reality, represented by the mallet and expressed by the underlying structures pushing the wooden bars together and out. It is, to reiterate, the first surface as an interface (between impression and expression) and, therefore, neither the first nor the last but the intermediate, ever the second even in its presumed self-commencement. Neither entirely inner nor outer, it is in its woodenness and vegetality a singular and finite gathering place for the infinity of elements, energies, flowing and stabilized in definite memorial forms. Rather than merely an intermediate layer, it is movement, shuttling between the inner and the outer with the rhythmicality Freud has signaled in his essay as the origin of the concept of time (SE 19: 231).

Now, the sphere of rhythmicality is primarily auditory. Time is first a rhythm, Freud implies, the rhythm of back-and-forth (*fort-da*) traversals of the space between the inner and the outer that, under the influence of these traversals, is temporalized, becomes time. Musicality is the self-consciousness of time, born of a rhythm. If so, then, in his strong negative reaction to music, which Jones describes, does Freud shy away from time as such, or, in a more nuanced way, does he do everything he can to prevent the imposition of other rhythms, other times (that are also the times of others) onto himself?

Freud's theory of time-consciousness is not so different from Husserl's, and the same goes for the shifting halo of attention and semi-attentiveness around intentionality as the motivated directedness-toward *this* rather than *that* target. For Freud, the rhythms of psychic life depend on the shifting configurations of cathexes shaping the system *Pcpt.-Cs.*, which, "cathected in this way, [. . .] receives perceptions (which are accompanied by consciousness) and passes the excitation to the unconscious mnemic systems; but as soon as the cathexis is withdrawn, consciousness is extinguished and the functioning of the system comes to a standstill (SE 19: 231).

Cathecting is striking the xylophone's wooden bars that pass the sound to the resonators and on to space, creating music and temporalizing this space, rhythmically. The stability and relative permanence of some cathexes is sustained resonance. But the singular binding of libidinal energy exceeds its immediate limits not only through the sound's diffusion in the surrounding space and perdurance in time. It a priori extends beyond itself in the material memory of the wood of the bars and in everything that co-sounds in their sounding: past solar blaze, decaying organic matter, and the fungal-bacterial-vegetal symbioses digesting it into the plant's body. The ego's cathexes are, then, both egoic and non-egoic. Disconnected from and connected to the unconscious and "external reality," the rhythms of their kindling and extinguishing, their binding and withdrawal, are ecological. *That* is xylophone magic.

Y

Yes-saying: affirmation and the limits of analysis

Freud's views on negation are well known. A *no* uttered by an analysand in therapy is not to be taken at face value; the stronger and the more passionate the denial of a proposed interpretation, the more evidence this negation supplies of the obverse in an equally strong unconscious resistance to the analytic finding. The analyst must not give in to the analysand's own assertion, but say *no* to this *no* and seek to lift residual resistances. This is what analysis—psycho-analysis, for sure, but not only it—shares with the quintessentially modern approaches to thinking itself, including radical doubt, critique, or the hermeneutics of suspicion.

I have already shown how Freud's approach to negation informs what may be termed "negative ecology." But what about affirmation, a yes-saying, which is perhaps still more difficult for an analyst to deal with, because it cannot be fully accommodated within the logic and the logistics of analysis?

In a late paper, "Constructions in Analysis" (1937), Freud puts the analysand's *no*s and *yes*es on the same footing. The entire paper is, in fact, concerned with giving an account of "how we are accustomed to arrive at an assessment of the 'Yes' or 'No' of our patients during analytic treatment" (SE 23: 257). Freud's main point is that the difference between affirmation and negation is negligible compared to sheer indifference, the analysand's neutral attitude discernible in a reaction "with neither a 'Yes' nor a 'No'" (SE 23: 261). In lieu of either negation or affirmation, it is this indifferent reaction that is an indication of a mistaken construction in analysis, that is to say, of a wrong *re*construction of the repressed materials that present themselves in the distortions of symptoms, dreams, free associations, etc. Evidently, the neutrality of a response bespeaks the absence of cathexes to the idea that is put forward as a therapeutic hypothesis, while both a *yes* and a *no* are charged with definite quanta of libidinal energy.

This is, nonetheless, the precise place where analysis reaches its limit, insofar as it is unable to proceed any further than the postulate of the formal equality of negation and affirmation. It cannot, for instance, take the side of the unconscious, which knows no *no*, or, differently put (and this difference is significant: Freud himself never resorts to such a positive description), which knows only *yes* in an unconditional affirmation of its desire. In fact, Freud will tackle (still by means of a double negative) the affirmative nature of the unconscious in papers on metapsychology, but not in his writings on the method of analytic practice nor in the many case studies he reports. Here is one such metapsychological formulation: "What we call our 'unconscious'—the deepest strata of our minds, made up of instinctual impulses—knows nothing that is negative, and no negation" (SE 14: 296).

Adding to the sense of asymmetry between the *yes* and the *no* in analysis are the disparate reasons for the reversion of each of these terms into the other. As Freud mentions in the Dora case, a certain formulation of the analysand's response translates a conscious *no* into an unconscious *yes*: "There is another very remarkable and entirely trustworthy form of confirmation from the unconscious, which I had not recognized at the time when this was written: namely, an exclamation on the part of the patient of 'I didn't think that', or 'I didn't think of that'. This can be translated point-blank into: 'Yes, I was unconscious of that'" (SE 7: 57). He reiterates the idea in the 1937 essay, where the statement "I didn't ever think . . ." is said to be translatable "without any hesitation into: 'Yes, you are right this time—about my *unconscious*'" (SE 23: 263). On the contrary, a *yes* that is not a *yes* dips into the unconscious no further than the resistances and other defense mechanisms that play the role of psychic gatekeepers.

Neither analysis nor any other modern methodological proposals for thinking I have mentioned are equipped for dealing with positivity without the mediations and the primacy (conceptual-epistemological *and* ontological) of negation. But what if more is going on in the case of an affirmation than analysis, in the guise of psycho-analysis, running up against its inherent limits? What if a related problem is raised by the materials it works with and conceptualizes as "constructions" (*Konstructionen*) that, in their elementary form, boil down to *yes* and *no*?

To speak of negation and affirmation before "construction" and, *ipso facto*, before the analyses of construction (structuralism is lurking just behind the corner here, and I wonder where deconstruction would fit within this scheme of things, given that it strives toward an absolute yes-saying, as Derrida's later texts suggest: would it still imply unpicking the existing constructions or would it lodge itself prior to the logic, or the articulation, of construction?) is not to slide into the mysterious, the unarticulated, and the inarticulate. Bachelard took the *yes* and the *no* antecedent to verbalizations and to the outcomes of human decisions to be the responses of the earth, of matter itself, of materials (whether they are organic or inorganic) that give in to external pressure or resist and counteract this pressure. A Freudian variation on the theme is not materialist, but ecological, bursting through the seams of the essay on, precisely, "constructions" in analysis.

As in his other works, Freud pursues the analogy between an analyst and an archeologist in their work of reconstructing psychic and material edifices by relying on fragments or traces. The "work of construction," he writes, "or, if it is preferred of reconstruction, resembles to a great extent an archaeologist's excavation of some dwelling-place that has been destroyed or buried or of some ancient edifice" (SE 23: 259). He goes on to assert that "the two processes are in fact identical" before shattering his own analogy in a move that can only derive from something other than the analytic drive: after all, what the analyst "is dealing with is not something destroyed but [. . .] is still alive" (SE 23: 259). Archeology and psychoanalysis share an intense interest in buildings, their partial disappearance and reconstruction, but in the case of the unconscious, Freud suggests, we are dealing with a living psychic edifice (or, at least, one that "is still alive"). The boundaries between building-ruining and growing-decaying have never been more blurred. We should not stop at these blurred boundaries, which are the upside of the purely negative limits of analysis, but proceed to inquire into the meaning of an edifice that is alive.

When archeology studies ancient shards and scattered building blocks, partially preserved mosaics or frescoes, broken columns and incomplete foundations, it engages with the material remnants of dwelling—not with dwelling itself. Filling in the gaps, ever so probabilistically, it aims to reconstruct (interpretatively, hermeneutically) the sense of dwelling that is no longer. It is a sense that is, at the same time, economic and ecological, branching out into every conceivable notion of *oikos*, "dwelling." Psychoanalysis, by comparison, deals with a living dwelling as an ongoing construction site, busy with its foundations that are never left behind altogether, reconstructed over and over again—that is, revived *and* deadened. The dwelling is given *and* withdrawn, entirely there over and above itself in the time synthesis of its chronologically distinct stages and always incomplete, such that construction (psychoanalytically understood) is not "a preliminary labor in the sense that the whole of it must be completed before the next piece of work [i.e., interpretation, MM] can be begun, as for instance, in the case of housebuilding, where all the walls must be erected and all the windows inserted before the internal decoration of the rooms can be taken in hand" (SE 23: 260). We inhabit it while it is still not objectively ready to be inhabited, and it is vacated while it still welcomes its inhabitants.

The dwelling and the construction site are, of course, the unconscious and the morsels of its translation—and mistranslation—into the terms of conscious psychic life. To be sure, one dwells unconsciously in oneself and in the world, but the unconscious itself is a strange dwelling, which is what the *yes* prior to the constructions of *yes* and *no*, *yes* or *no*, says at bottom. It is the kind of dwelling where one is outside or beside oneself within oneself, being the most foreign to one's (conscious) self at one's very core. This dwelling is always ready for habitation and it is never ready: though one is outside oneself in it, the unconscious knows no exteriority, no passage of time, no death. That is, finally, what a *yes* without and prior to a *no*, as well as prior to any affirmative *construction*, sounds and looks like. (*Nota bene*: the distinction between metaphysical concepts and the unconscious becomes exceedingly problematic here, once again!)

What about psychoanalysis and *its* relation to the purely affirmative *yes* on the hither side of positive and negative constructions? In the most condensed formulation conceivable, I would suggest that *analysts strain to listen to and analyze the non-analyzable*. For instance, psychoanalysis seeks the marks of repetition—"the repetitions of reactions dating from infancy" (SE 23: 259)—in order to shed light on them and to substitute them with other, more appropriate, more mature reactions. Habituation gives signs of itself by way of habituality, but the old habits that are "still living," that outlive their limited timespan when they were appropriate (or adaptive, in the evolutionary jargon), may be deadening. Then, it would have been better if they, themselves, were already dead and buried. This, however, is impossible, because, no matter how deeply one buries certain things in the unconscious, they spawn tentacular effects, which may be more or less disruptive to one's conscious life. That is why it is necessary to repeat whatever one has been repeating *otherwise*, to give its due to the primordial *yes*, to placate it and, simultaneously, to change a few vital elements in the repeated routines.

The analytic reconstruction inherent in the work of negative and positive constructions is a paradoxical revival of what is undead, "*still* living" despite . . . (is there an end to the possibilities of interpreting this *still*?). Freud recognizes, nevertheless, that the source of constructions in analysis—that is, really, of the propositional *yes* and *no* antecedent to interpretation—is the analyst and that, moreover, "the path that starts from the analyst's construction ought to end in the patient's recollection" (SE 23: 265). His prescription touches upon the matter of psychic dwelling, while raising two distinct possibilities. 1) Do analysts invite analysands to inhabit and to make their own the constructions that, while admittedly being work in progress, derive from the other? If that is what's going on, then we are dealing with psychological suggestion and false memories in excess of screen memories, which Freud is actually not so quick to discount altogether. Or: 2) Do analysts urge analysands to discern in the constructions proposed to them as it were from elsewhere something that had been a part of them, or that they have been a part of, all along—habitually and without knowing it, that is to say, uncannily?

Objectively and subjectively, the difference between these two options is enormous, but analytically and methodologically speaking it is not as big as it appears at first glance. Both options extend an invitation to the analysand to dwell together, to co-dwell before and beyond constructions in analysis, to cohabit in or to co-inhabit the absolute *yes*, which doesn't mean a simple acquiescence with the content of what is repeated, but, rather, going along with the repetition in order to repeat it otherwise. Traditional truth claims are inapplicable to the experience of an affirmative psychoanalytical ecology that pushes the boundaries of analysis, just as the effectiveness of constructions in therapy is not to be found in their acceptance or rejection at face value by the analysand but in their capacity to elicit a powerful reaction, be it positive or negative.

The economy of *yes* or *no*, *yes* and *no*, *yes* as *no*, and so forth in analytic constructions ought to be contrasted to the ecology of the *yes*, which motivates, diverts, rearranges, perverts, and thwarts these constructions. At the limits of analysis, the ecology of an absolute affirmation plays a role that is analogous to Kant's critique of reason, inasmuch as, from a position that is neither inside nor outside, it demarcates the terrain for the endless "preliminary labor" of interpreting or building. Freud's thought and practice hover *at* these limits, preoccupied with the economy of constructions but reaching back (and forward) to their ecological source, listening to the *yes*es and the *no*s so as to hear in them an echo of the absolute *yes* of the unconscious, the *yes* that is the unconscious.

Z

Zoophilia vs. zoephilia

While references to zoophilia in Freud's oeuvre are infrequent, they are undeniably consequential. In the January 11, 1897, letter to Fliess, Freud shares one of his two "red-hot" ideas based on recent analytic findings. "The perversions," he writes there, "regularly lead into zoophilia, and have an animal character. They are explained not by the functioning of erotogenic zones which has later been abandoned, but by the operations of erotogenic *sensations* which lose this force later. In this connection it will be recalled that the principal sense in animals (for sexual as well as other purposes) is that of smell, which has lost that position in human beings. So long as smell (or taste) is dominant, hair, feces, and the whole surface of the body—and blood as well—have a sexually exciting effect" (SE 1: 241).

In these early reflections, Freud does not conceive of zoophilia as one among many types of perversions but as something much broader than that. Aside from the fact that an other-than-human animal is the object of the sexual instinct in zoophilia, the perversions as such "have an animal character," which is to say that they are instigated by a certain reassertion of human animality. Zoophilia thus functions as a singular universal, a type of perversion, which, despite (and through) its singularity, embodies the universal it participates in.

The seemingly eccentric conclusion Freud reaches with regard to zoophilia has to do with his focus on "erotogenic *sensations*," instead of the erotogenic *zones* of the body, and especially on the sexually significant sense of smell. The volatility of olfactory substances cannot be circumscribed to this or that area of the body, or to things outside the organism, whence they emanate. Smell surrounds and goes beyond "the whole surface of the body," attaining a level of generality (of impression, of a feeling, of an atmospheric or ambient sense), which perhaps exceeds even touch, dispersed throughout the entire skin. This diffuse character of smell, which, as Freud observes, is an exceptionally important sense for animal sexuality and other purposes, puts it on a par with polymorphous perversity, whereby the body as a whole is saturated with sexual significance and energy. At the same time, the specificity of smell and its connection to animality do not amount to the sort of un- or non-differentiation implied in polymorophous perversity, which is why zoophilia attains such a status in Freud's analysis of perversions.

Not all animals, of course, are guided by their acute sense of smell, like dogs and many other mammals. Less than a biological fact, this Freudian generalization creates an implicit contrast between sexualization via olfaction and visually mediated sexuality with its scopophilic predilection already predominant in early childhood researches. Once again, the reference to "erotogenic *sensations*" is as misleading as it is revealing, because not all sensations are born equal: under this heading, Freud examines how smell subverts (or perverts) vision and its separation from, as well as control over, the image of the desired other. But, since "perversions regularly lead to zoophilia," the subversion of the visual by a deeper, enveloping, uncontrollable olfactory erotogenic sensation has something to do with the overall character of perversions and their recovery of animal sexuality in the human.

Freud will return to the question of zoophilia in *Three Essays*, where he will discuss, among other things, the sexual aberrations pertaining to "sexually immature persons and animals as sexual objects." He will point out in this text that "a light is thrown on the nature of the sexual instinct by the fact that it permits of so much variation in its objects and such a cheapening of them— which hunger, with its far more energetic retention of its objects, would only permit in the most extreme instances. A similar consideration applies to sexual intercourse with animals, which is by no means rare, especially among country people, and in which sexual attraction seems to override the barriers of species" (SE 7: 148).

Comparing sexual instinct to hunger, Freud reverts to the Aristotelian notion of the psyche, namely *to threptikon*, or vegetal vitality, with its capacities to be nourished and to reproduce that persist in all forms of life. In a certain sense, *to threptikon* is also perverse, and the same may be asserted about it as about zoophilia itself: it "seems to override the barriers of species." This perversion inherent to life itself—the vivifying and *re*vivifying perversion, if we dare imagine it from the standpoint of inorganic existence—is also that of the instinct prior to the ramification of its trajectories into preferred objects. And, according to Freud, of the two portions of the "life instinct," it is sexuality that is open to a greater variation, including a "cheapening" of the object, which would not have been possible except for the instances of extreme hunger in the case of nourishment.[1]

Toward the end of the passage I have cited, Freud comments on the fact that "sexual intercourse with animals [...] is by no means rare, especially among country people." This argument works in favor of the image of sexuality Freud presents throughout *Three Essays* to the effect that the aims and objects of sexual instinct are highly occasional, variable, plastic. So, it would appear that physical proximity to animals in everyday life invites their inclusion among sexual objects in an opportunistic (circumstances-, time- and place-dependent) key. Could it be, though, that the opposite situation of distancing from other-than-human animals, of urban alienation from the countryside, would similarly lead to the development of zoophilic tendencies, precisely in an attempt to overcome that separation in the most unsublimated fashion? Could there be something like "compensatory zoophilia," hypothetically more often relegated to the register of phantasy, as opposed to actual practice, alongside what I have termed, paraphrasing Freud, "opportunistic zoophilia"?

After all, in the earlier, if similarly cursory, treatment of the subject, Freud emphasizes that "perversions regularly lead into zoophilia," irrespective of where one finds oneself. Such non-differentiation among places must be further qualified: the sense of smell, which activates sexual desire bound to animality—our own and that of other-than-human animals—is more pronounced on a farm than in the more aseptic environments and is, therefore, linked not only to the organismic body and its odorous excretions but also to the microatmospheres of the places these bodies inhabit. The ecological component of zoophilia is the invisible frame for the aesthetic-sensory and biological-species aspects of the perversion (and, following Freud's train of thought, of perversion as such). Still, the generality of zoophilia, both mentioned and unmentioned by Freud, begs the question: Why does it overwhelm systems of classification—of species *and* of perversions, as the "regular" endpoint of the latter?

One obvious answer is that, in a non-sublimated manner, zoophilia acknowledges and affirms the uneasy persistence of other-than-human animality in the human. Smell puts us on the same footing as or even below other animals, mostly mammals, who have a sharper olfactory sense, which is crucial for discernments to do with sex and food alike. Scales and gradations, universes of meaning, bonds of attraction and forces of repulsion change as soon as they are approached from the olfactory domain. When Freud lists the predominance of everything that smells ("hair, feces, and the whole surface of the body"), he mixes together fetishes (hair), psychosexual fixations (feces), and polymorphous perversity (the whole surface of the body), bringing sexuality *tout court* into the mix. Momentarily, smell disorganizes and reorganizes the entire sexual ontology of the human, who is not only human.

In a similar vein, what the isolated perversion of zoophilia betrays—at once reveals and upsets—is a *zoephilia*, the love of *zoe*, "life" in its animalistic dimension. It is this life that is subject to severe repression, complementing alienation from the other-than-human animals outside of us with a separation from the animal within.[2] In keeping with my provisional categorization of its sundry forms, compensatory zoophilia compensates, precisely, for the blockages of zoephilia, while opportunistic zoophilia expresses zoephilia in an unsublimated fashion. Empathic identification with animals and keeping them as pets are the sublimated versions of the same impulse.

From a patchwork of suggestions in Freud's writings dating back to the first decade of the twentieth century, it is possible to reconstruct his allegiance to what I have termed "zoephilia." While his (predominantly male) patients will display all kinds of animal phobias, Freud advocates sexual education at schools, highlighting the affinities between humans and animals also with respect to sexuality. So, in "The Sexual Enlightenment of Children," he writes: "It is the duty of schools not to evade the mention of sexual matters. The main facts of reproduction and their significance should be included in lessons about the animal kingdom, and at the same time stress should be laid on the fact that man shares everything essential in his organization with the higher animals" (SE 9: 138). This is the obverse of the joint treatment of zoophilia and pedophilia in the treatise on sexuality from 1905 (*Three Essays*) published only two years prior to the open letter on "sexual enlightenment": children have an easier time identifying with other-than-human animals because their psychological defense mechanisms and the apparatus of repression still do not go into overdrive, with the exception of extreme phobias. Sexual enlightenment is achieved not by repressing the animality of human sexual life but by appreciating, through a study of analogous structures and functions, "everything essential" that is shared with higher animals.

In a 1908 text, "The Sexual Theories of Children," Freud confirms the affinities between children and animals on matters of sexuality, notably when it comes to the rejection of "the stork fable" of childbirth. "It is the child's observation of animals, who hide so little of their sexual life and to whom he feels so closely akin, that strengthens his disbelief in it [i.e., in the stork fable, MM]" (SE 9: 215). Nothing less than the fate of thinking is at stake in such learning from animals—a zoephilic learning, one might say—which is also why Freud resorts to the term "enlightenment," *Aufklärung*, rather than "education," in his advocacy of introducing topics related to sexuality in school curricula. "With his knowledge, independently obtained," Freud explains, "that babies grow inside the mother's body, he would be on the right road to solving the problem on which he first tries out his powers of thinking" (SE 9: 215).

Mediated by animals, sexual enlightenment morphs into enlightenment as such, the capacity to observe, test hypotheses, solve problems, exercise the "powers of thinking" with regard to causes and effects. The independent acquisition of knowledge does not mean that the sexual researcher child reaches correct conclusions in a purely autonomous manner; it simply refers to the fact that the child is not going to be told a tall tale and take it at face value. The initial steps on the path of the enlightenment, as much sexual as it is general (and here we are reminded of the unavoidable conflation of the singular and the universal affecting a specific perversion and perversion as such, or vegetal vitality and psychic life as a whole), are guided by animals, who, more than the objects of observation, are subjects and to whom a child "feels so closely akin."

Counterintuitive as this may sound, Freud nevertheless deems human sexuality to be more intensive *and* more extensive than animal sexuality, factoring in all the sublimations of libidinal energy in the former: "The sexual instinct [. . .] is probably more strongly developed in man than in most of the higher animals; it is certainly more constant, since it has almost entirely overcome its periodicity to which it is tied in animals. It places extraordinarily large amounts of force at the disposal of civilized activity, and it does this in virtue of its especially marked characteristic of being able to displace its aim without materially diminishing its intensity" (SE 9: 187).

The overcoming of periodicity in human sexual instinct is tantamount to the overcoming of time itself, unthinkable without the rhythms of periodic alternations and alterations (of day and night, of the seasons, and even of the regular intervals between time's more abstract measures: seconds, minutes, hours). Human sexuality, then, adheres to the model of the unconscious that knows no passage of time, including in its highly "civilized," sublimated manifestations. What renders it unique is the seemingly endless variations in the displaced sexual aims, originally decoupled from the "purposes of reproduction" and having as their goal "the gaining of particular kinds of pleasure" (SE 9: 188). Zoophilia is one such displacement, extracted from the reproductive order without sublimation, onto other-than-human animals. Zoephilia, in turn, is a sublimated displacement onto non-sublimated life, and it is for this reason that it runs the risk of idealization, of reimagining this life as equally sublimated all the way down.

Notes

Preface

1 See Naomi Klein, *This Changes Everything: Capitalism and the Climate* (New York: Simon & Schuster, 2014).

2 For more on this, consult Michael Marder, *Energy Dreams: Of Actuality* (New York: Columbia University Press, 2017).

3 Freud makes this point in his writings on "metapsychology." This and all subsequent quotes from his oeuvre, refer to Sigmund Freud, *The Standard Edition of the Complete Psychological Works of Sigmund Freud*, 24 volumes, translated and edited by James Strachey (London: Vintage, 2001). Henceforth, Standard Edition volumes will be cited as "SE" followed by volume and page numbers.

4 Santiago Zabala, "Imagining a Philosophy of Warnings for Our Greatest Emergency." *Philosophy Today*, 64(4), Fall 2020, pp. 1–5; Santiago Zabala, *Signs from the Future: A Philosophy of Warnings* (New York: Columbia University Press, 2025).

5 Refer to Michael Marder and Santiago Zabala, "De la filosofía de la advertencia al pensamento ecológico." Forthcoming in 2026.

6 Cosimo Schinaia, *Psychoanalysis and Ecology: The Unconscious and the Environment* (Abingdon & New York: Routledge, 2022).

7 Michael Marder, *The Phoenix Complex: A Philosophy of Nature* (Cambridge, MA: MIT Press, 2023).

A Anxious states

1 Caroline Hickman et al., "Climate anxiety in children and young people and their beliefs about government responses to climate change: a global survey." *Lancet Planetary Health* 5(12), December 2021. <https://www.thelancet.com/journals/lanplh/article/PIIS2542-5196(21)00278-3/fulltext>

2 See also SE 20: 129: "Symptoms are created so as to avoid the generating of anxiety."

3 "The high degree of narcissistic value which the penis possesses can appeal to the fact that that organ is a guarantee to its owner that he can be once more united to his mother—i.e., to a substitute for her—in the act of copulation" (SE 20: 139).

B Biodiversity conundrums (with an eye to the death drive)

1 Sabina Spielrein, "Destruction as the Cause of Coming into Being." *Journal of Analytical Psychology*, 39, 1994[1912], pp. 155–86. <https://aphelis.net/wp-content/uploads/2012/05/SPIELREIN_1912_Destruction_as_cause_of_coming_into_being.pdf>

D Dump, defecation

1 Michael Marder, *Dump Philosophy: A Phemonenology of Devastation* (London: Bloomsbury, 2020), pp. 81ff.

E Environment, "external world," eco-psycho-analysis

1 Further discussion of this feature may be found in Michael Marder, *Time Is a Plant* (Leiden: Brill, 2023).

2 Refer to Sally Weintrobe, "The Climate Crisis." In *Routledge Handbook of Psychoanalytic Political Theory*, edited by Yannis Stavrakakis (London & New York: Routledge, 2019).

3 "The reactions to seeing the Earth from space make manifest tensions between nationalism and cosmopolitanism and between humanism, in the sense that we are the center of the universe, and posthumanism, in the sense that we are insignificant in the universe. In these reactions to seeing the Earth, there are contradictory urges to both love it and leave it" (Kelly Oliver, *Earth & World: Philosophy after the Apollo Missions* [New York: Columbia University Press, 2015], p. 15).

F Fetishism and the climate

1 Timothy Morton, *Hyperobjects: Philosophy and Ecology after the End of the World* (Minneapolis: University of Minnesota Press, 2013).

G Geo-psycho-analysis

1 Jacques Derrida, *Psyche: Invention of the Other*, vol. 1, edited by Peggy Kamuf and Elizabeth Rottenberg (Stanford: Stanford University Press, 2007), p. 319.

2 In already existing geological hollows, the caves, we witness symbolic fluidity between the phallus and the fetus much discussed in psychoanalysis and instigating the movement of separation, of birth, or rebirth.

3 Kelly Oliver, *Earth and World: Philosophy after the Apollo Missions* (New York: Columbia University Press, 2015).

4 Elon Musk, "Making Humanity an Interplanetary Species." *SpaceX*, September 28, 2016. <https://www.youtube.com/watch?v=H7Uyfqi_TE8>

H Hysteric conversions between organismic and ecological bodies

1 One may argue that Arendt's theory of natality and political philosophy as a whole are anti-hysterical.

2 H. T. Alborn et al., "An Elicitor of Plant Volatiles from Beet Armyworm Oral Secretion." *Science* 276(5314), 1997, pp. 945–9. <https://www.science.org/doi/10.1126/science.276.5314.945>

3 O. Falik et al., "Root navigation by self-inhibition." *Plant, Cell & Environment*, 28(4), 2005, pp. 562–9.

4 In hi-tec and knowledge-based economies, strikes lose their effectiveness, since the main asset here is connectivity, both online and physical. The exception of an effective strike in this situation is by workers employed in the means of transport or those ensuring the proper functioning of the internet.

I Inhibitions: of ecological thinking and/in action

1 Slavoj Žižek, *Revolution at the Gates: Selected Writings of Lenin from 1917* (London & New York: Verso, 2011), p. 306.

K Kissing and knowing

1 Refer to the final chapter, "Kisses," in Michael Marder, *Green Mass: The Ecological Theology of St. Hildegard of Bingen* (Stanford: Stanford University Press, 2021).

2 In a psychoanalytic vein, it is utterly legitimate to inquire whether or not every *materialism* is not idealized, allowing the materialist to overcome disgust.

L Libidinal ecologies

1 Philippe Lynes, *Futures of Life Death on Earth: Derrida's General Ecology* (London: Rowman & Littlefield, 2018).

M Melancholy variations

1 Renée Lertzman, *Environmental Melancholia: Psychoanalytic Dimensions of Engagement* (New York & London: Routledge, 2015), p. xiii.

2 Cosimo Schinaia, *Psychoanalysis and Ecology: The Unconscious and the Environment* (Abingdon & New York, 2022), p. 90.

3 Judith Butler, *Precarious Life: The Powers of Mourning and Violence* (London & New York: Verso, 2004), p. xiv.

4 See Michael T. Moore and David M. Fresco, "Depressive Realism: A Meta-Analytic Review." *Clinical Psychology Review*, 32(6), August 2012, pp. 496–509.

N Negative ecology

1 "What we call our 'unconscious'—the deepest strata of our minds, made up of instinctual impulses—knows nothing that is negative, and no negation; in it, contradictories coincide. For that reason, it does not know its own death, for to that we can give only a negative content. Thus, there is nothing instinctual in us which responds to a belief in death" (SE 14: 296).

O Obsessive self-blame

1 Probably, the denial and repression by representatives of the first group fan the flames of excessive self-blame by those who fall into the second group.

Q Queer ecology, Freud-style

1 "The normal sexual aim is *regarded as* being the union of the genitals in the act known as copulation [...]," (SE 7: 149) Freud writes when introducing deviations of the sexual aim. This formulation is not fortuitous. Before tackling deviations of the sexual object, Freud invokes "the relation between these deviations and *what is assumed to be normal*" (SE 7: 136). Emphasis mine in both cases.

R Rats, horses, wolves, and other animals

1 Oxana Timofeeva, *Freud's Beasty Boys: Sex, Violence and Masculinity* (Cambridge: Polity Press, 2025). Many of the observations in this chapter are in dialogue with Timofeeva's virtuoso treatment of the cases involving animals, animality, and animalization in Freud's practice.

2 Refer to "Introduction: Rhizome," in Gilles Deleuze and Felix Guattari, *A Thousand Plateaus: Capitalism and Schizophrenia*, translated by Brian Massumi (Minneapolis: University of Minnesota Press, 1987).

S Sadism and the sentience of other-than-human beings

1 Michael Marder, "If Peas Can Talk, Should We Eat Them?" *New York Times*, April 28, 2012. <https://archive.nytimes.com/opinionator.blogs.nytimes.com/2012/04/28/if-peas-can-talk-should-we-eat-them/>

2 That is, incidentally, the psychological—not the purely philosophical or class—reason for the dialectical superiority of the slave position vis-à-vis the master in the struggle for recognition and the emergence of self-consciousness, as Hegel depicts it in *Phenomenology of Spirit*.

T Trauma extensions

1 Refer to Michael Marder, *Fabrication: Of Intelligence and Nature. A Philosophical Fugue*. Forthcoming in 2026.

2 Suffice it to say, on the subject of the dump's extension beyond planetary confines, that the dimension of the problem is now cosmic, given the massive quantities of non-decomposing space junk orbiting the Earth.

3 Marder, *Dump Philosophy*, passim.

U Uncanniness: leaving, coming back home, and leaving again with ecology

1   For the logic behind divine doubling, see Charles Stang, *Our Divine Double* (Cambridge, MA: Harvard University Press, 2016).

V Vultures, kites, and other ani-things

1   Oliver Slow, "Mona Lisa: Protesters Throw Soup at da Vinci Painting." *BBC News*, January 28, 2024. <https://www.bbc.com/news/world-europe-68121654>

X Xylophone magic: echoes and eco's

1   Ernest Jones, *The Life and Work of Sigmund Freud*, vol. 1. (New York: Basic Books, 1953), pp. 17–18.

2   Jacques Derrida, *The Ear of the Other: Otobiography, Transference, Translation*, translated by Peggy Kamuf (Lincoln, NE: University of Nebraska Press, 1988), p. 33.

3   For more on a phenomenological interpretation of sound/sounds, see Marcia Cavalcante Schuback, "Rhythm and Existence," *Research in Phenomenology*, (48)3, 2018, pp. 318–30.

Z Zoophilia vs. zoephilia

1   Empirically speaking, the relation to objects is inverted in sexuality and the nutritive drive: the latter, by and large, entails eating the other of another species or biological kingdom, whereas the former, also by and large, occasions attraction to a member of one's own biological species.

2   In this sense, the thesis of Mary Midgley's *Beast and Man: The Roots of Human Nature* (London & New York: Routledge, 2002) remains unsurpassable.*NotesNotes*